ALSO BY EVE ENSLER

Necessary Targets

The Good Body

Insecure at Last

EDITED BY EVE ENSLER
AND MOLLIE DOYLE

A Memory, a Monologue,
a Rant, and a Prayer

THE
VAGINA
MONOLOGUES

THE VAGINA MONOLOGUES

Eve Ensler

VILLARD

NEW YORK

2008 Villard Books Trade Paperback Edition

Copyright © 1998, 2008 by Eve Ensler
Foreword copyright © 1998 by Gloria Steinem

Published in the United States by Villard Books, an imprint of
The Random House Publishing Group, a division of
Random House, Inc., New York.

VILLARD and "V" CIRCLED Design are registered trademarks of
Random House, Inc.

Earlier editions of this work were originally published in hardcover in
1998 and in trade paperback in 2001 by Villard Books, an imprint of
The Random House Publishing Group, a division of Random House,
Inc. This 10th Anniversary edition has been simultaneously published
in hardcover by Villard Books, an imprint of The Random House
Publishing Group, a division of Random House, Inc.

Originally produced by HOME for Contemporary Theatre and Art
at HERE, Randy Rollison, artistic director, and Barbara Busackino,
producing director, in association with Wendy Evans Joseph.
Produced Off-Broadway by David Stone, Willa Shalit, Nina
Essman, Dan Markley/Mike Skipper, and the Araca Group.

Library of Congress Cataloging-in-Publication Data
Ensler, Eve.
The vagina monologues / Eve Ensler.
p. cm.
ISBN 0-345-49860-1
1. Monologues.   2. Vagina.   3. Women.
PS3555.N75V3   2001
812'.54—dc21   00-043844

Printed in the United States of America

www.villard.com

2 4 6 8 9 7 5 3 1

Book design by Caroline Cunningham

For Ariel, who rocked my vagina

and exploded my heart

IN MEMORY

To my dear friend Bob Fennell,

who protected me and brought me forward.

I miss you.

INTRODUCTION TO THE TENTH ANNIVERSARY EDITION

It is hard to believe that almost fifteen years have passed since I first said the word "vagina" on a small stage in a little theater called HERE in downtown New York City. When I first read these monologues, my most pressing concern was being able to get the words out of my terrified mouth. I certainly could not have conceived then what would follow in terms of both a movement to end violence against women and girls, and the life of

The Vagina Monologues itself. I had no intention of even writing a play. I was already a way way downtown playwright. I assumed a play about vaginas would permanently secure that status.

If I have learned anything in these last fifteen years, it is how to hold two opposite thoughts at the same time. The most radical play I had ever written turned out to be the play that was accepted and invited into the mainstream. Saying the word I was not supposed to say is the thing that gave me a voice in the world. Revealing the very personal stories of women and their private parts gave birth to a public, global movement to end violence against women and girls called V-Day.

In terms of existing in the world of opposites, I see now that living between *The Vagina Monologues* and the V-Day movement, between the ambiguous energy of theater and the less nuanced world of activism, has both stretched and inspired me. The art has made the activism more creative and bold, the activism has made the art more sharply focused, more grounded, more dangerous. The trick in both has been to avoid ideology and fundamentalism in one direction, fragmentation and irresponsibility in the other. The trick has been to lay a certain groundwork—i.e., the play, the intention of the movement—and then to trust individuals and groups to bring their own vision, culture, and creativity to the experience. The trick has been to create something that is both concrete and fluid, something that can spread quickly and yet has integrity, something that is owned and changed by many and has certain ingredients and laws that allow this adaptability. The trick has been to live in the contradictions while maintaining principles, beliefs, and purpose.

I believe this friction has been at the core of what has energized and spread V-Day so quickly around the world. The excitement and danger of speaking the word, of performing the play in tiny villages or conservative cities, with unlikely performers (ministers and doctors and telephone workers and members of parliament) and in unusual venues (churches and synagogues, women's living rooms, stadiums, factories), has propelled the play to be performed in 45 languages and 119 countries, raising nearly $50 million through grassroots efforts to end violence against women and girls.

There have been so many victories. Women speaking the word where it had never been uttered. Women standing up against local and national governments, religious forces, parents, husbands, friends, university administrators, college presidents, and the voices inside them that judge and censor. College students across the world making V-Day a radical annual event (it's been noted that there are two things on every college campus, a Starbucks and a V-Day). Women reclaiming their bodies and telling the stories of their own violations, desires, victories, shame, adventures. Women finding their power, their voice, and their leadership ability by becoming "accidental activists." Women finding one another, standing up for women in other parts of the world, releasing memories that have numbed their bodies and depleted their energy. Women standing onstage, on edge, in reds and pinks, with New York accents, southern accents, African accents, Indian accents, and British accents. Speaking, screaming, whispering, laughing, and moaning.

There are so many tales, so many images. A group of about thirty Comfort Women* between the ages of seventy and ninety chanting *"PUKI"* (pronounced "pook-ee," which means "vagina" in Tagalog) with their fists raised. Most had never said the word in their entire life. The president of Iceland declaring himself a Vagina Warrior. Hundreds of girls in Kenya dancing in the African sun as the first V-Day safe house opens, ensuring protection from having their clitorises cut. A Catholic girls' school in Cap Haitien overflowing with more than five hundred people, packed with enthusiastic men talking back to the performers. An armed, sirened motorcade in Port au Prince, Haiti, traveling through the streets, with STOP

*See footnote page 176.

VIOLENCE AGAINST WOMEN signs on all the cars. Nurses at the Panzi Hospital in Bukavu in the Democratic Republic of the Congo reading *The Vagina Monologues,* releasing Congolese moans on a rooftop. Women in Islamabad, Pakistan, dressed in red salwar kameez and saris, performing for their sisters who were there from Afghanistan— everyone laughing and weeping. Thousands in the streets of Ciudad Juárez, coming from all over the world, standing up at the V-Day march to stop the murders and mutilation of women. Mary Alice, the brilliant New York actor, taking down the Apollo in Harlem with her orgasms at the first V-Day celebrating African American, Asian, and Latina women and girls. A fourteen-hour bus ride to Himachal Pradesh in India to open a sanctuary for women. The mayor of Rome opening the V-Day Summit there. A walk through a seven-foot vagina in the lobby of the San Francisco V-Day. "My Vagina Was My Village," the monologue about a raped Bosnian woman, being performed at the UN, at Madison Square Garden, in Bosnia by college students who were there during the war, at the Royal Albert Hall, in Johannesburg, Macedonia, Athens. A seven-language performance of the monologues in Brussels, during the V-Day European Summit. The word "vagina" standing out as the only English word in an Arabic article written in the *Beirut Times.* Red feathers being handed out at the Indian Country production of the play in Rapid City. Learning to sign "clitoris" in a performance by deaf women in Washington, D.C. Vagina T-shirts, lollipops, buttons, quilts, puppets, panties, posters, votes, attitudes, and style.

So much has happened. So much has changed. We can now point to places where violence has been reduced or has been stopped altogether or where the consciousness has most clearly shifted. We have had huge victories.

Then, of course, there is the opposite. The world is still profoundly unsafe for women. Violence escalates. War abounds.

In the last year, during V-Day's Spotlight on

Women in Conflict Zones, I traveled to Haiti and the Democratic Republic of Congo. I visited women in cities throughout the U.S. and Europe. I met with our V-Day sisters from Egypt, Jordan, Morocco, Iraq, Lebanon, and Afghanistan.

In Haiti I found that rape, a tool used in the war there, is now essentially normalized and rampant—so much so that hundreds of women report rapes each and every month.

In the Democratic Republic of Congo, I heard the soul-cracking and heinous stories of atrocities toward women: sexual torture and raping of hundreds of thousands of women and girls.

Throughout North America and Europe, I am still hearing the stories of women being raped in colleges, beaten in their homes, trafficked and sold in the streets.

In Iraq, there has been a rampant destruction of women's rights since the U.S. invasion, a rise in honor killings, rapes, and murders of women.

In Afghanistan, warlords, rapists, and murderers are in power, the Taliban are coming back, girls are afraid to go to school, women teachers are being murdered, outspoken women in parliament threatened and censored.

In Egypt and throughout Africa, women are still genitally cut—nearly two million a year.

We have broken through many barriers, we have changed the landscape of the dialogue, we have reclaimed our stories and our voices, but we have not yet unraveled or deconstructed the inherent cultural underpinnings and causes of violence. We have not penetrated the mindset that, somewhere in every single culture, gives permission to violence, expects violence, waits for violence, and instigates violence. We have not stopped teaching boys to deny being afraid, doubtful, needy, sorrowful, vulnerable, open, tender, and compassionate.

We have not yet elected or become leaders who refuse violence as a possible intervention, who make ending violence the purpose of all we do, rather than amassing more weapons and proving how macho and unbending we can be. We have not elected or become leaders who understand that you cannot say you believe in protecting women and children and then support bombing Iraq. Exactly whose children do you believe in protecting? We have not yet elected or become leaders who understand that the mechanisms of occupation, domination, and invasion operating on an international level also influence and direct what happens in the home on a domestic level. We have not elected or become leaders who are brave enough to make ending violence against women the central issue of our campaign or office.

We have not yet made violence against women abnormal, extraordinary, unacceptable. We have not cracked the tectonic plate at the center of the human psyche that is more terrified to love than to kill.

If we are going to end violence against women, the whole story has to change. We have to look at shame and humiliation and poverty and racism and what building an empire on the back of the world does to the people who are bent over. We have to say that what happens to women matters to everyone and it matters A LOT.

Even raising money to stop violence against women makes it something other, something separate from the human condition, from every moment of our daily lives. It creates a strange fragmentation and an even more bizarre fiction. We will give three million dollars to stop rape. We concretize what is abstract and integral because we need to raise money and people feel better giving money to things: a safe house in Africa, a workshop in Jordan, a hospital for women in the Democratic Republic of the Congo. And so we have constructed an antiviolence movement that has created shelters and hotlines and places for women to run to be safe. And although these places are crucial to ensuring women's safety, they keep the focus on things or places rather than the issue, on rescue rather than transformation.

It is the culture that has to change—the beliefs, the underlying story and behavior of the culture.

Ending violence against women is not a form of altruism or something you do as a charitable act. It is not something you can even legislate, although laws help to protect women and change thinking and behavior.

I have said from the beginning that ending violence against women cannot be the thing we get to later. Somehow governments, world bodies like the UN, foundations, and local and world leaders have still not made this issue a priority, have not stepped up front and center with the energy, resources, and will to make a difference. We are still, all these years later, fighting for crumbs— morally, politically, financially. V-Day now raises more money than any group in the world to stop violence against women. This is not good news. In one year we raise four to six million dollars. That is the cost of ten minutes of the war in Iraq. One out of three women on the planet will be beaten or raped. You do the math.

Women are not some marginalized, insignificant group. We are more than half of the world's citizens. What happens to us determines everything. If we are beaten and traumatized, our children will hold that in their DNA and grow up manifesting that in who they become. If our esteem is destroyed, our daughters' self-confidence will be hard won or impossible to come by. If we are violated and raped or abused by men, our sons will be made in the witnessing of this, and in our bitterness.

Ending violence against women is actually about each of us being willing to struggle to be a different kind of human being. It means not accepting force as a method of coercion and oppression—in our homes and in our world. But really it means examining what is at the root of that need for force. Why are women still muted, controlled, silenced, weakened, and contained? What would happen if they were safe and free?

Ending violence against women means opening to the great power of women, the mystery of women, the heart of women, the wild, unending sexuality and creativity of women—and not being afraid.

Eve Ensler ·
September 2007

CONTENTS

FOREWORD

by Gloria Steinem

I come from the "down there" generation. That is, those were the words—spoken rarely and in a hushed voice—that the women in my family used to refer to all female genitalia, internal or external.

It wasn't that they were ignorant of terms like *vagina, labia, vulva,* or *clitoris.* On the contrary, they were trained to be teachers and probably had more access to information than most.

It wasn't even that they were unliberated, or "straitlaced," as they would have put it. One grandmother earned money from her strict Protestant church by ghostwriting sermons—of which she didn't believe a word—and then earned more by betting it on horse races. The other was a suffragist, educator, and even an early political candidate, all to the alarm of many in her Jewish community. As for my own mother, she had been a pioneer newspaper reporter years before I was born, and continued to take pride in bringing up her two daughters in a more enlightened way than she had been raised. I don't remember her using any of the slang words that made the female body seem dirty or shameful, and I'm grateful for that. As you'll see in these pages, many daughters grew up with a greater burden.

Nonetheless, I didn't hear words that were accurate, much less prideful. For example, I never once heard the word *clitoris.* It would be years before I learned that females possessed the only organ in the human body with no function other than to feel pleasure. (If such an organ were unique to the male body, can you imagine how much we would hear about it—and what it would be used to justify?) Thus, whether I was learning to talk, to spell, or to take care of my own body, I was told the name of each of its amazing parts—except in one unmentionable area. This left me unprotected against the shaming words and dirty jokes of the school yard and, later, against the popular belief that men, whether as lovers or physicians, knew more about women's bodies than women did.

I first glimpsed the spirit of self-knowledge and freedom that you will find in these pages when I lived in India for a couple of years after college. In Hindu temples and shrines I saw the lingam, an abstract male genital symbol, but I also saw the yoni, a female genital symbol, for the first time: a flowerlike shape, triangle, or double-pointed oval. I was told that thousands of years ago, this symbol had been worshiped as more powerful than its male counterpart, a belief that carried over into Tantrism, whose central tenet is man's inability to reach spiritual fulfillment except through sexual and emotional union with woman's superior spiritual energy. It was a belief so deep and wide that even some of the woman-excluding, monotheistic religions that came later retained it in their traditions, although such beliefs were (and still are) marginalized or denied as heresies by mainstream religious leaders.

For example: Gnostic Christians worshiped Sophia as the female Holy Spirit and considered Mary Magdalene the wisest of Christ's disciples; Tantric Buddhism still teaches that Buddhahood resides in the vulva; the Sufi mystics of Islam believe that *fana,* or rapture, can be reached only through Fravashi, the female spirit; the Shekina of Jewish mysticism is a version of Shakti, the female soul of God; and even the Catholic church included forms of Mary worship that focused more on the Mother than on the Son. In many countries of Asia, Africa, and other parts of the world where gods are still depicted in female as well as in male forms, altars feature the Jewel in the Lotus and other representations of the lingam-in-the-yoni. In India, the Hindu goddesses Durga and Kali are embodiments of the yoni powers of birth and death, creation and destruction.

Still, India and yoni worship seemed a long way from American attitudes about women's bodies when I came home. Even the sexual revolution of the 1960s only made more women sexually available to more men. The "no" of the 1950s was just replaced with a constant, eager "yes." It was not until the feminist activism of the 1970s that there began to be alternatives to everything from patriarchal religions to Freud (the distance from A to B), from the double standard of sexual behavior to the single standard of patriarchal/political/religious control over women's bodies as the means of reproduction.

Those early years of discovery are symbolized for me by such sense memories as walking through Judy Chicago's *Woman House* in Los Angeles, where each room was created by a different woman artist, and where I discovered female symbolism in my own culture for the first time. (For example, the shape we call a heart—whose symmetry resembles the vulva far more than the asymmetry of the organ that shares its name—is probably a residual female genital symbol. It was reduced from power to romance by centuries of male dominance.) Or sitting in a New York coffee shop with Betty Dodson (you will meet her in these pages), trying to act cool while she electrified eavesdroppers with her cheerful explanation of masturbation as a liberating force. Or coming back to *Ms.* magazine to find, among the always humorous signs on its bulletin board: IT'S 10 O'CLOCK AT NIGHT—DO YOU KNOW WHERE YOUR CLITORIS IS? By the time feminists were putting CUNT POWER! on buttons and T-shirts as a way of reclaiming that devalued word, I could recognize the restoration of an ancient power. After all, the Indo-European word *cunt* was derived from the goddess Kali's title of Kunda or Cunti, and shares the same root as *kin* and *country*.

These last three decades of feminism were also marked by a deep anger as the truth of violence against the female body was revealed, whether it took the form of rape, childhood sexual abuse, anti-lesbian violence, physical abuse of women, sexual harassment, terrorism against reproductive freedom, or the international crime of female genital mutilation. Women's sanity was saved by bringing these hidden experiences into the open, naming them, and turning our rage into positive action to reduce and heal violence. Part of the tidal wave of creativity that has resulted from this energy of truth telling is this play and book.

When I first went to see Eve Ensler perform the intimate narratives in these pages—gathered from more than two hundred interviews and then turned into poetry for the theater—I thought: *I already know this: it's the journey of truth telling we've been on for the past three decades.* And it is. Women have entrusted her with their most intimate experiences, from sex to birthing, from the undeclared war against women to the new freedom of love between women. On every page, there is the power of saying the unsayable—as there is in the behind-the-scenes story of the book itself. One publisher paid an advance for it, then, on sober second thought, allowed Eve Ensler to keep the money if she would take the book and its v-word elsewhere. (Thank Villard for publishing all of the women's words—even in the title.)

But the value of *The Vagina Monologues* goes beyond purging a past full of negative attitudes. It offers a personal, grounded-in-the-body way of moving toward the future. I think readers, men as well as women, may emerge from these pages not only feeling more free within themselves—and about each other—but with alternatives to the old patriarchal dualism of feminine/masculine, body/ mind, and sexual/spiritual that is rooted in the division of our physical selves into "the part we talk about" and "the part we don't."

If a book with *vagina* in the title still seems a long way from such questions of philosophy and politics, I offer one more of my belated discoveries.

In the 1970s, while researching in the Library of Congress, I found an obscure history of religious architecture that assumed a fact as if it were common knowledge: the traditional design of most patriarchal buildings of worship imitates the female body. Thus, there is an outer and inner entrance, labia majora and labia minora; a central vaginal aisle toward the altar; two curved ovarian structures on either side; and then in the sacred center, the altar or womb, where the miracle takes place—where males give birth.

Though this comparison was new to me, it struck home like a rock down a well. *Of course,* I thought. *The central ceremony of patriarchal religions is one in which men take over the yoni-power of creation by giving birth symbolically. No wonder male religious leaders so often say that humans were born in sin— because we were born to female creatures. Only by obeying the rules of the patriarchy can we be reborn through men. No wonder priests and ministers in skirts sprinkle imitation birth fluid over our heads, give us new names, and promise rebirth into everlasting life. No wonder the male priesthood tries to keep women away from the altar, just as women are kept away from control of our own powers of reproduction. Symbolic or real, it's all devoted to controlling the power that resides in the female body.*

Since then, I've never felt the same estrangement when entering a patriarchal religious structure. Instead, I walk down the vaginal aisle, plotting to take back the altar with priests—female as well as male—who would not disparage female sexuality, to universalize the male-only myths of Creation, to multiply spiritual words and symbols, and to restore the spirit of God in all living things.

If overthrowing some five thousand years of patriarchy seems like a big order, just focus on celebrating each self-respecting step along the way.

I thought of this while watching little girls drawing hearts in their notebooks, even dotting their *i*'s with hearts, and I wondered: *Were they magnetized by this primordial shape because it was so like their own bodies?* I thought of it again while listening to a group of twenty or so diverse nine- to sixteen-year-old girls as they decided to come up with a collective word that included everything—vagina, labia, clitoris. After much discussion, "power bundle" was their favorite. More important, the discussion was carried on with shouts and laughter. I thought: *What a long and blessed way from a hushed "down there."*

I wish my own foremothers had known their bodies were sacred. With the help of outrageous voices and honest words like those in this book, I believe the grandmothers, mothers, and daughters of the future will heal their selves—and mend the world.

"Vagina." There, I've said it. "Vagina"—said it again. I've been saying that word over and over for the last three years. I've been saying it in theaters, at colleges, in living rooms, in cafés, at dinner parties, on radio programs all over the country. I would be saying it on TV if someone would let me. I say it one hundred and twenty-eight times every evening I perform my show, *The Vagina Monologues,* which is based on interviews with a diverse group of over two hundred women about their vaginas. I say it in my sleep. I say it because I'm not supposed to say it. I say it because it's an invisible word—a word that stirs up anxiety, awkwardness, contempt, and disgust.

I say it because I believe that what we don't say we don't see, acknowledge, or remember. What we don't say becomes a secret, and secrets often create shame and fear and myths. I say it because I want to someday feel comfortable saying it, and not ashamed and guilty.

I say it because we haven't come up with a word that's more inclusive, that really describes the entire area and all its parts. "Pussy" is probably a better word, but it has so much baggage connected with it. And besides, I don't think most of us have a clear idea of what we're talking about when we say "pussy." "Vulva" is a good word; it speaks more specifically, but I don't think most of us are clear what the vulva includes.

I say "vagina" because when I started saying it I discovered how fragmented I was, how disconnected my body was from my mind. My vagina was something over there, away in the distance. I rarely lived inside it, or even visited. I was busy working, writing; being a mother, a friend. I did not see my vagina as my primary resource, a place of sustenance, humor, and creativity. It was fraught there, full of fear. I'd been raped as a little girl, and although I'd grown up, and done all the adult things one does with one's vagina, I had never really reentered that part of my body after I'd been violated. I had essentially lived most of my life without my motor, my center, my second heart.

I say "vagina" because I want people to respond, and they have. They have tried to censor the word wherever *The Vagina Monologues* has traveled and in every form of communication: in ads in major newspapers, on tickets sold in department stores, on banners that hang in front of theaters, on box-office phone machines where the voice says only "Monologues" or "V. Monologues."

"Why is this?" I ask. " 'Vagina' is not a pornographic word; it's actually a medical word, a term for a body part, like 'elbow,' 'hand,' or 'rib.' "

"It may not be pornographic," people say, "but it's dirty. What if our little daughters were to hear it, what would we tell them?"

"Maybe you could tell them that they have a vagina," I say. "If they don't already know it. Maybe you could celebrate that."

"But we don't call their vaginas 'vagina,' " they say.

"What do you call them?" I ask.

And they tell me: "pooki," "poochie," "poope," "peepe poopelu" . . . and the list goes on and on.

I say "vagina" because I have read the statistics, and bad things are happening to women's vaginas everywhere: 500,000 women are raped every year in the United States; 100 million women have been genitally mutilated worldwide; and the list goes on and on. I say "vagina" because I want these bad things to stop. I know they will not stop until we acknowledge that they're going on, and the only way to make that possible is to enable women to talk without fear of punishment or retribution.

It's scary saying the word. "Vagina." At first it feels like you're crashing through an invisible wall. "Vagina." You feel guilty and wrong, as if someone's going to strike you down. Then, after you say the word the hundredth time or the thousandth time, it occurs to you that it's *your* word, *your* body, *your* most essential place. You suddenly realize that all the shame and embarrassment you've previously felt saying the word has been a form of silencing your desire, eroding your ambition.

Then you begin to say the word more and more. You say it with a kind of passion, a kind of urgency, because you sense that if you stop saying it, the fear will overcome you again and you will fall back into an embarrassed whisper. So you say it everywhere you can, bring it up in every conversation.

You're excited about your vagina; you want to study it and explore it and introduce yourself to it, and find out how to listen to it, and give it pleasure, and keep it healthy and wise and strong. You learn how to satisfy yourself and teach your lover how to satisfy you.

You're aware of your vagina all day, wherever you are—in your car, at the supermarket, at the gym, in the office. You're aware of this precious, gorgeous, life-bearing part of you between your legs, and it makes you smile; it makes you proud.

And as more women say the word, saying it becomes less of a big deal; it becomes part of our language, part of our lives. Our vaginas become integrated and respected and sacred. They become part of our bodies, connected to our minds, fueling our spirits. And the shame leaves and the violation stops, because vaginas are visible and real, and they are connected to powerful, wise, vagina-talking women.

We have a huge journey in front of us.

This is the beginning. Here's the place to think about our vaginas, to learn about other women's vaginas, to hear stories and interviews, to answer questions and to ask them. Here's the place to release the myths, shame, and fear. Here's the place to practice saying the word, because, as we know, the word is what propels us and sets us free. "VAGINA."

THE
VAGINA
MONOLOGUES

I bet you're worried. *I* was worried. That's why I began this piece. I was worried about vaginas. I was worried about what we think about vaginas, and even more worried that we don't think about them. I was worried about my own vagina. It needed a context of other vaginas—a community, a culture of vaginas. There's so much darkness and secrecy surrounding them—like the

Bermuda Triangle. Nobody ever reports back from there.

In the first place, it's not so easy even to find your vagina. Women go weeks, months, sometimes years without looking at it. I interviewed a high-powered businesswoman who told me she was too busy; she didn't have the time. Looking at your vagina, she said, is a full day's work. You have to get down there on your back in front of a mirror that's standing on its own, full-length preferred. You've got to get in the perfect position, with the perfect light, which then is shadowed somehow by the mirror and the angle you're at. You get all twisted up. You're arching your head up, killing your back. You're exhausted by then. She said she didn't have the time for that. She was busy.

So I decided to talk to women about their vaginas, to do vagina interviews, which became vagina monologues. I talked with over two hundred women. I talked to older women, young women, married women, single women, lesbians, college professors, actors, corporate professionals, sex workers, African American women, Hispanic women, Asian American women, Native American women, Caucasian women, Jewish women. At first women were reluctant to talk. They were a little shy. But once they got going, you couldn't stop them. Women secretly love to talk about their vaginas. They get very excited, mainly because no one's ever asked them before.

Let's just start with the word "vagina." It sounds like an infection at best, maybe a medical instrument: "Hurry, Nurse, bring me the vagina." "Vagina." "Vagina." Doesn't matter how many times you say it, it never sounds like a word you want to say. It's a totally ridiculous, completely unsexy word. If you use it during sex, trying to be politically correct—"Darling, could you stroke my vagina?"—you kill the act right there.

I'm worried about vaginas, what we call them and don't call them.

In Great Neck, they call it a pussycat. A woman there told me that her mother used to tell her, "Don't wear panties underneath your pajamas, dear; you need to air out your pussycat." In Westchester they called it a pooki, in New Jersey a twat. There's "powderbox," "derrière," a "poochi," a "poopi," a "peepe," a "poopelu," a "poonani," a "pal" and a "piche," "toadie," "dee dee," "nishi," "dignity," "monkey box," "coochi snorcher," "cooter," "labbe," "Gladys Siegelman," "VA," "wee wee," "horsespot," "nappy dugout," "mongo," a "pajama," "fannyboo," "mushmellow," a "ghoulie," "possible," "tamale," "tottita," "Connie," a "Mimi" in Miami, "split knish" in Philadelphia, and "schmende" in the Bronx. I am worried about vaginas.

Some of the monologues are close to verbatim interviews, some are composite interviews, and with some I just began with the seed of an interview and had a good time. This monologue is pretty much the way I heard it. Its subject, however, came up in every interview, and often it was fraught. The subject being

H A I R

You cannot love a vagina unless you love hair.
Many people do not love hair. My first and only
husband hated hair. He said it was cluttered and
dirty. He made me shave my vagina. It looked
puffy and exposed and like a little girl. This excited him. When he made love to me, my vagina
felt the way a beard must feel. It felt good to rub
it, and painful. Like scratching a mosquito bite. It
felt like it was on fire. There were screaming red

bumps. I refused to shave it again. Then my hus-band had an affair. When we went to marital ther-apy, he said he screwed around because I wouldn't please him sexually. I wouldn't shave my vagina. The therapist had a thick German accent and gasped between sentences to show her empathy. She asked me why I didn't want to please my hus-band. I told her I thought it was weird. I felt little when my hair was gone down there, and I couldn't help talking in a baby voice, and the skin got irri-tated and even calamine lotion wouldn't help it. She told me marriage was a compromise. I asked her if shaving my vagina would stop him from screwing around. I asked her if she'd had many cases like this before. She said that questions di-luted the process. I needed to jump in. She was sure it was a good beginning.

This time, when we got home, he got to shave my vagina. It was like a therapy bonus prize. He clipped it a few times, and there was a little blood in the bathtub. He didn't even notice it, 'cause he was so happy shaving me. Then, later, when my husband was pressing against me, I could feel his spiky sharpness sticking into me, my naked puffy vagina. There was no protection. There was no fluff.

I realized then that hair is there for a reason—it's the leaf around the flower, the lawn around the house. You have to love hair in order to love the vagina. You can't pick the parts you want. And besides, my husband never stopped screwing around.

I asked all the women I interviewed the same ques-
tions and then I picked my favorite answers. Although I
must tell you, I've never heard an answer I didn't love.
I asked women:

"If your vagina got dressed, what would it wear?"

A beret.

A leather jacket.

Silk stockings.

Mink.

A pink boa.

A male tuxedo.

Jeans.

Something formfitting.

Emeralds.

An evening gown.

Sequins.

Armani only.

A tutu.

See-through black underwear.

A taffeta ball gown.

Something machine washable.

Costume eye mask.

Purple velvet pajamas.

Angora.

A red bow.

Ermine and pearls.

A large hat full of flowers.

A leopard hat.

A silk kimono.

Glasses.

Sweatpants.

A tattoo.

An electrical shock device to keep unwanted
strangers away.

High heels.

Lace *and* combat boots.

Purple feathers and twigs and shells.

Cotton.

A pinafore.

A bikini.

A slicker.

"If your vagina could talk, what would it say, in two words?"

Slow down.

Is that you?

Feed me.

I want.

Yum, yum.

Oh, yeah.

Start again.

No, over there.

Lick me.

Stay home.

Brave choice.

Think again.

More, please.

Embrace me.

Let's play.

Don't stop.

More, more.

Remember me?

Come inside.

Not yet.

Whoah, Mama.

Yes yes.

Rock me.

Enter at your own risk.

Oh, God.

Thank God.

I'm here.

Let's go.

Let's go.

Find me.

Thank you.

Bonjour.

Too hard.

Don't give up.

Where's Brian?

That's better.

Yes, there. There.

I interviewed a group of women between the ages of sixty-five and seventy-five. These interviews were the most poignant of all, possibly because many of the women had never had a vagina interview before. Unfortunately, most of the women in this age group had very little conscious relationship to their vaginas. I felt terribly lucky to have grown up in the feminist era. One woman who was seventy-two had never even seen her vagina. She had only touched herself when she was

*washing in the shower, but never with conscious inten-
tion. She had never had an orgasm. At seventy-two she
went into therapy, and with the encouragement of her
therapist, she went home one afternoon by herself, lit
some candles, took a bath, played some comforting
music, and discovered her vagina. She said it took her
over an hour, because she was arthritic by then, but
when she finally found her clitoris, she said, she cried.
This monologue is for her.*

THE FLOOD

[Jewish, Queens accent]

Down there? I haven't been down there since 1953. No, it had nothing to do with Eisenhower. No, no, it's a cellar down there. It's very damp, clammy. You don't want to go down there. Trust me. You'd get sick. Suffocating. Very nauseating. The smell of the clamminess and the mildew and everything. Whew! Smells unbearable. Gets in your clothes.

No, there was no accident down there. It

didn't blow up or catch on fire or anything. It wasn't so dramatic. I mean . . . well, never mind. No. Never mind. I can't talk to you about this. What's a smart girl like you going around talking to old ladies about their down-theres for? We didn't do this kind of a thing when I was a girl. What? Jesus, okay.

There was this boy, Andy Leftkov. He was cute—well, I thought so. And tall, like me, and I really liked him. He asked me out for a date in his car. . . .

I can't tell you this. I can't do this, talk about down there. You just know it's there. Like the cellar. There's rumbles down there sometimes. You can hear the pipes, and things get caught there, little animals and things, and it gets wet, and sometimes people have to come and plug up the leaks. Otherwise, the door stays closed. You forget about it. I mean, it's part of the house, but you don't see it or think about it. It has to be there, though, 'cause every house needs a cellar. Otherwise the bedroom would be in the basement.

Oh, Andy, Andy Leftkov. Right. Andy was very good-looking. He was a catch. That's what we called it in my day. We were in his car, a new white Chevy BelAir. I remember thinking that my legs were too long for the seat. I have long legs. They were bumping up against the dashboard. I was looking at my big kneecaps when he just kissed me in this surprisingly "Take me by control like they do in the movies" kind of way. And I got excited, so excited, and, well, there was a flood down there. I couldn't control it. It was like this force of passion, this river of life just flooded out of me, right through my panties, right onto the car seat of his new white Chevy BelAir. It wasn't pee and it was smelly—well, frankly, I didn't really smell anything at all, but he said, Andy said, that it smelled like sour milk and it was staining his car seat. I was "a stinky weird girl," he said. I wanted to explain that his kiss had caught me off guard, that I wasn't normally like this. I tried to wipe the flood up with my dress. It was a new yellow prim-rose dress and it looked so ugly with the flood on it. Andy drove me home and he never, never said another word and when I got out and closed his car door, I closed the whole store. Locked it. Never opened for business again. I dated some after that, but the idea of flooding made me too nervous. I never even got close again.

I used to have dreams, crazy dreams. Oh, they're dopey. Why? Burt Reynolds. I don't know why. He never did much for me in life, but in my dreams . . . it was always Burt and I. Burt and I. Burt and I. We'd be out. Burt and I. It was some restaurant like the kind you see in Atlantic City, all big with chandeliers and stuff and thousands of waiters with vests on. Burt would give me this orchid corsage. I'd pin it on my blazer. We'd laugh. We were always laughing, Burt and I. Eat shrimp cocktail. Huge shrimp, fabulous shrimp. We'd laugh more. We were very happy together. Then he'd look into my eyes and pull me to him in the middle of the restaurant—and, just as he was about to kiss me, the room would start to shake, pigeons would fly out from under the table—I don't know what those pigeons were doing there—and the flood would come straight from down there. It would pour out of me. It would pour and pour. There would be fish inside it, and little boats, and the whole restaurant would fill with water, and Burt would be standing knee-deep in my flood, looking horribly disappointed in me that I'd done it again, horrified as he watched his friends, Dean Martin and the like, swim past us in their tuxedos and evening gowns.

I don't have those dreams anymore. Not since they took away just about everything connected with down there. Moved out the uterus, the tubes, the whole works. The doctor thought he was being funny. He told me if you don't use it, you lose it. But really I found out it was cancer. Everything around it had to go. Who needs it, anyway? Right? Highly overrated. I've done other things. I love the dog shows. I sell antiques.

What would it wear? What kind of question is that? What would it wear? It would wear a big sign:

"Closed Due to Flooding."

What would it say? I told you. It's not like that. It's not like a person who speaks. It stopped being a thing that talked a long time ago. It's a place. A place you don't go. It's closed up, under the house. It's down there. You happy? You made me talk—you got it out of me. You got an old lady to talk about her down-there. You feel better now? [Turns away; turns back.]

You know, actually, you're the first person I ever talked to about this, and I feel a little better.

At a witch trial in 1593, the investigating lawyer (a married man) apparently discovered a clitoris for the first time; [he] identified it as a devil's teat, sure proof of the witch's guilt. It was "a little lump of flesh, in manner sticking out as if it had been a teat, to the length of half an inch," which the gaoler, "perceiving at the first sight thereof, meant not to disclose, because it was adjoining to so secret a place which was not decent to be seen. Yet in the end, not willing to conceal so strange a matter," he showed it to various by-standers. The bystanders had never seen anything like it. The witch was convicted.

—*The Woman's Encyclopedia of Myths and Secrets*

I interviewed many women about menstruation. There was a choral thing that began to occur, a kind of wild collective song. Women echoed each other. I let the voices bleed into one another. I got lost in the bleeding.

I WAS TWELVE. MY MOTHER SLAPPED ME.

Second grade, seven years old, my brother was talking about periods. I didn't like the way he was laughing.

I went to my mother. "What's a period?" I said. "It's punctuation," she said. "You put it at the end of a sentence."

My father brought me a card: "To my little girl who isn't so little anymore."

I was terrified. My mother showed me the

thick sanitary napkins. I was to bring the used ones to the can under the kitchen sink.

I remember being one of the last. I was thirteen.

We all wanted it to come.

I was so afraid. I started putting the used pads in brown paper bags in the dark storage places under the roof.

Eighth grade. My mother said, "Oh, that's nice."

In junior high—brown drips before it came. Coincided with a little hair under my arms, which grew unevenly: one armpit had hair, the other didn't.

I was sixteen, sort of scared.

My mother gave me codeine. We had bunk beds. I went down and lay there. My mother was so uncomfortable.

One night, I came home late and snuck into bed without turning on any lights. My mother had found the used pads and put them between the sheets of my bed.

I was twelve years old, still in my under-pants. Hadn't gotten dressed. Looked down on the staircase. There it was.

Looked down and I saw blood.

Seventh grade; my mother sort of noticed my underwear. Then she gave me plastic diapers.

My mom was very warm—"Let's get you a pad."

My friend Marcia, they celebrated when she got hers. They had dinner for her.

We all wanted our period.

We all wanted it *now*.

Thirteen years old. It was before Kotex. Had to watch your dress. I was black and poor. Blood on the back of my dress in church. Didn't show, but I was guilty.

I was ten and a half. No preparation. Brown gunk on my underpants.

She showed me how to put in a tampon. Only got in halfway.

I associated my period with inexplicable phe-nomena.

My mother told me I had to use a rag. My mother said no to tampons. You couldn't put anything in your sugar dish.

Wore wads of cotton. Told my mother. She gave me Elizabeth Taylor paper dolls.

Fifteen years old. My mother said, "Mazel tov." She slapped me in the face. Didn't know if it was a good thing or a bad thing.

My period, like cake mix before it's baked. Indians sat on moss for five days. Wish I were Native American.

I was fifteen and I'd been hoping to get it. I was tall and I kept growing.

When I saw white girls in the gym with tampons, I thought they were bad girls.

Saw little red drops on the pink tiles. I said, "Yeah."

My mom was glad for me.

Used OB and liked putting my fingers up there.

Eleven years old, wearing white pants. Blood started to come out.

Thought it was dreadful.

I'm not ready.

I got back pains.

I got horny.

Twelve years old. I was happy. My friend had a Ouija board, asked when we were going to get our periods, looked down, and I saw blood.

Looked down and there it was.

I'm a woman.

Terrified.

Never thought it would come.

Changed my whole feeling about myself. I became very silent and mature. A good Vietnamese woman—quiet worker, virtuous, never speaks.

Nine and a half. I was sure I was bleeding to death, rolled up my underwear and threw them in a corner. Didn't want to worry my parents.

My mother made me hot water and wine, and I fell asleep.

I was in my bedroom in my mother's apartment. I had a comic book collection. My mother said, "You mustn't lift your box of comic books."

My girlfriends told me you hemorrhage every month.

My mother was in and out of mental hospitals. She couldn't take me coming of age.

"Dear Miss Carling, Please excuse my daughter from basketball. She has just matured."

At camp they told me not to take a bath with my period. They wiped me down with antiseptic.

Scared people would smell it. Scared they'd say I smelled like fish.

Throwing up, couldn't eat.

I got hungry.

Sometimes it's very red.

I like the drops that drop into the toilet. Like paint.

Sometimes it's brown and it disturbs me.

I was twelve. My mother slapped me and brought me a red cotton shirt. My father went out for a bottle of sangria.

*This is based on an interview I did with a woman
who had taken the Vagina Workshop.*

THE
VAGINA
WORKSHOP

[A slight English accent]

My vagina is a shell, a round pink tender shell, opening and closing, closing and opening. My vagina is a flower, an eccentric tulip, the center acute and deep, the scent delicate, the petals gentle but sturdy.

I did not always know this. I learned this in the vagina workshop. I learned this from a woman who runs the vagina workshop, a woman who believes in vaginas, who really sees vaginas, who helps women see their own vaginas by seeing other women's vaginas.

In the first session the woman who runs the vagina workshop asked us to draw a picture of our own "unique, beautiful, fabulous vagina." That's what she called it. She wanted to know what our own unique, beautiful, fabulous vagina looked like to us. One woman who was pregnant drew a big red mouth screaming with coins spilling out. Another very skinny woman drew a big serving plate with a kind of Devonshire pattern on it. I drew a huge black dot with little squiggly lines around it. The black dot was equal to a black hole in space, and the squiggly lines were meant to be people or things or just your basic atoms that got lost there. I had always thought of my vagina as an anatomical vacuum randomly sucking up particles and objects from the surrounding environment.

I had always perceived my vagina as an independent entity, spinning like a star in its own galaxy, eventually burning up on its own gaseous energy or exploding and splitting into thousands of other smaller vaginas, all of them then spinning in their own galaxies.

I did not think of my vagina in practical or biological terms. I did not, for example, see it as a part of my body, something between my legs, attached to me.

In the workshop we were asked to look at our vaginas with hand mirrors. Then, after careful examination, we were to verbally report to the group what we saw. I must tell you that up until this point everything I knew about my vagina was based on hearsay or invention. I had never really seen the thing. It had never occurred to me to look at it. My vagina existed for me on some abstract plane. It seemed so reductive and awkward to look at it, getting down there the way we did in the workshop, on our shiny blue mats, with our hand mirrors. It reminded me of how the early astronomers must have felt with their primitive telescopes.

I found it quite unsettling at first, my vagina.

Like the first time you see a fish cut open and you discover this other bloody complex world inside, right under the skin. It was so raw, so red, so fresh. And the thing that surprised me most was all the layers. Layers inside layers, opening into more layers.

My vagina amazed me. I couldn't speak when it came my turn in the workshop. I was speechless. I had awakened to what the woman who ran the workshop called "vaginal wonder." I just wanted to lie there on my mat, my legs spread, examining my vagina forever.

It was better than the Grand Canyon, ancient and full of grace. It had the innocence and freshness of a proper English garden. It was funny, very funny. It made me laugh. It could hide and seek, open and close. It was a mouth. It was the morning.

Then, the woman who ran the workshop asked how many women in the workshop had had orgasms. Two women tentatively raised their hands. I didn't raise my hand, but I had had orgasms. I didn't raise my hand because they were accidental orgasms. They happened *to* me. They happened in my dreams, and I would wake in splendor. They happened a lot in water, mostly in the bath. Once in Cape Cod. They happened on horses, on bicycles, on the treadmill at the gym. I did not raise my hand because although I had had orgasms, I did not know how to make one happen. I had never tried to make one happen. I thought it was a mystical, magical thing. I didn't want to interfere. It felt wrong, getting involved—contrived, manipulative. It felt Hollywood. Orgasms by formula. The surprise would be gone, and the mystery. The problem, of course, was that the surprise had been gone for two years. I hadn't had a magical accidental orgasm in a long time, and I was frantic. That's why I was in the workshop.

And then the moment had arrived that I both dreaded and secretly longed for. The woman who ran the workshop asked us to take out our hand mirrors again and to see if we could locate our clitoris. We were there, the group of us women, on our backs, on our mats, finding our spots, our locus, our reason, and I don't know why, but I started crying. Maybe it was sheer embarrassment. Maybe it was knowing that I had to give up the fantasy, the enormous life-consuming fantasy, that someone or something was going to do this for me—the fantasy that someone was coming to lead my life, to choose direction, to give me orgasms. I was used to living off the record, in a magical, superstitious way. This clitoris finding, this wild workshop on shiny blue mats, was making the whole thing real, too real. I could feel the panic coming. The simultaneous terror and realization that I had avoided finding my clitoris, had rationalized it as mainstream and consumerist because I was, in fact, terrified that I did not *have* a clitoris, terrified that I was one of those constitutionally incapables, one of those frigid, dead, shut-down, dry, apricot-tasting, bitter—oh, my God. I lay there with my mirror looking for my spot, reaching with my fingers, and all

I could think about was the time when I was ten and lost my gold ring with the emeralds in a lake. How I kept diving over and over to the bottom of the lake, running my hands over stones and fish and bottle caps and slimy stuff, but never my ring. The panic I felt. I knew I'd be punished. I shouldn't have worn it swimming.

The woman who ran the workshop saw my insane scrambling, sweating, and heavy breathing. She came over. I told her, "I've lost my clitoris. It's gone. I shouldn't have worn it swimming." The woman who ran the workshop laughed. She calmly stroked my forehead. She told me my clitoris was not something I could lose. It was me, the essence of me. It was both the doorbell to my house and the house itself. I didn't have to *find* it. I had to *be* it. Be it. Be my clitoris. Be my clitoris. I lay back and closed my eyes. I put the mirror down. I watched myself float above myself. I watched as I slowly began to approach myself and reenter. I felt like an astronaut reentering the atmosphere of the earth. It was very quiet, this reentry: quiet and gentle. I bounced and landed, landed and bounced. I came into my own muscles and blood and cells and then I just slid into my vagina. It was suddenly easy and I fit. I was all warm and pulsing and ready and young and alive. And then, without looking, with my eyes still closed, I put my finger on what had suddenly become me. There was a little quivering at first, which urged me to stay. Then the quivering became a quake, an eruption, the layers dividing and subdividing. The quaking broke open into an ancient horizon of light and silence, which opened onto a plane of music and colors and innocence and longing, and I felt connection, calling connection as I lay there thrashing about on my little blue mat.

My vagina is a shell, a tulip, and a destiny. I am arriving as I am beginning to leave. My vagina, my vagina, me.

The clitoris is pure in purpose. It is the only organ in the body designed purely for pleasure. The clitoris is simply a bundle of nerves: 8,000 nerve fibers, to be precise. That's a higher concentration of nerve fibers than is found anywhere else in the body, including the fingertips, lips, and tongue, and it is twice . . . twice . . . twice the number in the penis. Who needs a handgun when you've got a semiautomatic.

—from *Woman: An Intimate Geography,* by Natalie Angier

BECAUSE HE LIKED TO LOOK AT IT

This is how I came to love my vagina. It's embarrassing, because it's not politically correct. I mean, I know it should have happened in a bath with salt grains from the Dead Sea, Enya playing, me loving my woman self. I know the story. Vaginas are beautiful. Our self-hatred is only the internalized repression and hatred of the patriarchal culture. It isn't real. Pussys unite. I know all of it. Like, if we'd grown up in a culture where we were taught that fat thighs were beautiful, we'd all be pounding down milkshakes and cookies, lying on our backs, spending our days thigh-expanding. But we didn't grow up in that culture. I hated my thighs, and I hated my vagina even more. I thought it was incredibly ugly. I was one of those women who had looked at it and, from that moment on, wished I hadn't. It made me sick. I pitied anyone who had to go down there.

In order to survive, I began to pretend there was something else between my legs. I imagined furniture—cozy futons with light cotton comforters, little velvet settees, leopard rugs—or pretty things—silk handkerchiefs, quilted pot holders, or place settings—or miniature landscapes—clear crystal lakes or moisty Irish bogs. I got so accustomed to this that I lost all memory of having a vagina. Whenever I had sex with a man, I pictured him inside a mink-lined muffler or a red rose or a Chinese bowl.

Then I met Bob. Bob was the most ordinary man I ever met. He was thin and tall and nondescript and wore khaki clothes. Bob did not like spicy foods or listen to Prodigy. He had no interest in sexy lingerie. In the summer he spent time in the shade. He did not share his inner feelings. He did not have any problems or issues, and was not even an alcoholic. He wasn't very funny or articulate or mysterious. He wasn't mean or unavailable. He wasn't self-involved or charismatic. He didn't drive fast. I didn't particularly like Bob. I would have missed him altogether if he hadn't picked up my change that I dropped on the deli floor. When he handed me back my quarters and pennies and his hand accidentally touched mine, something happened. I went to bed with him. That's when the miracle occurred.

Turned out that Bob loved vaginas. He was a connoisseur. He loved the way they felt, the way they tasted, the way they smelled, but most important, he loved the way they looked. He had to look at them. The first time we had sex, he told me he had to see me.

"I'm right here," I said.

"No, you," he said. "I have to see you."

"Turn on the light," I said.

Thinking he was a weirdo, I was freaking out in the dark. He turned on the light.

Then he said, "Okay. I'm ready, ready to see you."

"Right here." I waved. "I'm right here."

Then he began to undress me.

"What are you doing, Bob?" I said.

"I need to see you," he replied.

"No need," I said. "Just dive in."

"I need to see what you look like," he said.

"But you've seen a red leather couch before," I said.

Bob continued. He would not stop. I wanted to throw up and die.

"This is awfully intimate," I said. "Can't you just dive in?"

"No," he said. "It's who you are. I need to look."

I held my breath. He looked and looked. He gasped and smiled and stared and groaned. He got breathy and his face changed. He didn't look ordinary anymore. He looked like a hungry, beautiful beast.

"You're so beautiful," he said. "You're elegant and deep and innocent and wild."

"You saw that there?" I said.

It was like he read my palm.

"I saw that," he said, "and more—much, much more."

He stayed looking for almost an hour, as if he were studying a map, observing the moon, staring into my eyes, but it was my vagina. In the light, I watched him looking at me, and he was so genuinely excited, so peaceful and euphoric, I began to get wet and turned on. I began to see myself the way he saw me. I began to feel beautiful and delicious—like a great painting or a waterfall. Bob wasn't afraid. He wasn't grossed out. I began to swell, began to feel proud. Began to love my vagina. And Bob lost himself there and I was there with him, in my vagina, and we were gone.

In 1993, I was walking down a street in Manhattan when I passed a newsstand and was suddenly struck by a deeply disturbing photograph on the front page of Newsday. *It was a picture of a group of six young women who had just been returned from a rape camp in Bosnia. Their faces revealed shock and despair, but more disturbing was a sense that something sweet, something pure, had been forever destroyed in each of their lives. I read on. Inside the newspaper was another photograph of the young women, recently reunited with their mothers and standing in a semicircle in a gymnasium. There was a very large group and not one of them, mother or daughter, was able to look at the camera.*

I knew I had to go there. I had to meet these women. In 1994, thanks to the support of an angel, Lauren Lloyd, I spent two months in Croatia and Pakistan, interviewing Bosnian women refugees. I interviewed these women and hung out with them in camps, cafés, and refugee centers. I have been back to Bosnia twice since then.

When I returned to New York after my first trip, I was in a state of outrage. Outraged that 20,000 to 70,000 women were being raped in the middle of Europe in 1993, as a systematic tactic of war, and no one was doing anything to stop it. I couldn't understand it. A friend asked me why I was surprised. She said that over 500,000 women were raped every year in this country, and in theory we were not at war.

This monologue is based on one woman's story. I want to thank her here for sharing it with me. I am in awe of her spirit and strength, as I am in awe of every woman I met who survived these terrible atrocities in the former Yugoslavia. This piece is for the women of Bosnia.

MY VAGINA WAS MY

VILLAGE

My vagina was green, water soft pink fields,
cow mooing sun resting sweet boyfriend touching
lightly with soft piece of blond straw.

*There is something between my legs. I do not know
what it is. I do not know where it is. I do not touch. Not
now. Not anymore. Not since.*

My vagina was chatty, can't wait, so much,
so much saying, words talking, can't quit trying,
can't quit saying, oh yes, oh yes.

Not since I dream there's a dead animal sewn in down there with thick black fishing line. And the bad dead animal smell cannot be removed. And its throat is slit and it bleeds through all my summer dresses.

My vagina singing all girl songs, all goat bells ringing songs, all wild autumn field songs, vagina songs, vagina home songs.

Not since the soldiers put a long thick rifle inside me. So cold, the steel rod canceling my heart. Don't know whether they're going to fire it or shove it through my spinning brain. Six of them, monstrous doctors with black masks shoving bottles up me too. There were sticks, and the end of a broom.

My vagina swimming river water, clean spilling water over sun-baked stones over stone clit, clit stones over and over.

Not since I heard the skin tear and made lemon screeching sounds, not since a piece of my vagina came off in my hand, a part of the lip, now one side of the lip is completely gone.

My vagina. A live wet water village. My vagina my hometown.

Not since they took turns for seven days smelling like feces and smoked meat, they left their dirty sperm inside me. I became a river of poison and pus and all the crops died, and the fish.

My vagina a live wet water village.
They invaded it. Butchered it and burned it
    down.
I do not touch now.
Do not visit.
I live someplace else now.
I don't know where that is.

In the nineteenth century, girls who learned to develop orgasmic capacity by masturbation were regarded as medical problems. Often they were "treated" or "corrected" by amputation or cautery of the clitoris or "miniature chastity belts," sewing the vaginal lips together to put the clitoris out of reach, and even castration by surgical removal of the ovaries. But there are no references in the medical literature to the surgical removal of testicles or amputation of the penis to stop masturbation in boys.

In the United States, the last recorded clitoridectomy for curing masturbation was performed in 1948—on a five-year-old girl.

—*The Woman's Encyclopedia of Myths and Secrets*

Genital mutilation has been inflicted on 80 [million] to 100 million girls and young women. In countries where it is practiced, mostly African, about 2 million youngsters a year can expect the knife—or the razor or a glass shard—to cut their clitoris or remove it altogether, [and] to have part or all of the labia . . . sewn together with catgut or thorns.

Often the operation is prettified as "circumcision." The African specialist Nahid Toubia puts it plain: In a man it would range from amputation of most of the penis, to "removal of all the penis, its roots of soft tissue and part of the scrotal skin."

Short-term results include tetanus, septicemia, hemorrhages, cuts in the urethra, bladder, vaginal walls, and anal sphincter. Long-term: chronic uterine infection, massive scars that can hinder walking for life, fistula formation, hugely increased agony and danger during childbirth, and early deaths.

—*The New York Times*, April 12, 1996

MY ANGRY VAGINA

My vagina's angry. It is. It's pissed off. My vagina's furious and it needs to talk. It needs to talk about all this shit. It needs to talk to you. I mean, what's the deal? An army of people out there thinking up ways to torture my poor-ass, gentle, loving vagina. . . . Spending their days constructing psycho products and nasty ideas to undermine my pussy. Vagina motherfuckers.

All this shit they're constantly trying to

shove up us, clean us up—stuff us up, make it go away. Well, my vagina's not going away. It's pissed off and it's staying right here. Like tampons— what the hell is that? A wad of dry fucking cotton stuffed up there. Why can't they find a way to subtly lubricate the tampon? As soon as my vagina sees it, it goes into shock. It says, Forget it. It closes up. You need to work with the vagina, in- troduce it to things, prepare the way. That's what foreplay's all about. You got to convince my vagina, seduce my vagina, engage my vagina's trust. You can't do that with a dry wad of fucking cotton.

Stop shoving things up me. Stop shoving and stop cleaning it up. My vagina doesn't need to be cleaned up. It smells good already. Not like rose petals. Don't try to decorate. Don't believe him when he tells you it smells like rose petals when it's supposed to smell like pussy. That's what they're doing—trying to clean it up, make it smell like bathroom spray or a garden. All those douche sprays—floral, berry, rain. I don't want my pussy to smell like rain. All cleaned up like washing a fish after you cook it. Want to *taste* the fish. That's why I ordered it.

Then there's those exams. Who thought them up? There's got to be a better way to do those exams. Why the scary paper dress that scratches your tits and crunches when you lie down so you feel like a wad of paper someone threw away? Why the rubber gloves? Why the flashlight all up there like Nancy Drew working against gravity, why the Nazi steel stirrups, the mean cold duck lips they shove inside you? What's that? My vagina's angry about those visits. It gets defended weeks in advance. It shuts down, won't "relax." Don't you hate that? "Relax your vagina, relax your vagina." Why? My vagina's not stupid. Relax so you can shove those cold duck lips inside it? I don't think so.

Why can't they find some nice, delicious purple velvet and wrap it around me, lay me down on some feathery cotton spread, put on some nice, friendly pink or blue gloves, and rest my feet in some fur-covered stirrups? Warm up the duck lips. Work with my vagina.

But no, more tortures: dry wad of fucking cotton, cold duck lips, and thong underwear. That's the worst. Thong underwear. Who thought that up? Moves around all the time, gets stuck in the back of your vagina, real crusty butt.

Vagina's supposed to be loose and wide, not held together. That's why girdles are so bad. We need to move and spread and talk and talk. Vaginas need comfort. Make something like that, something to give them pleasure. No, of course they won't do that. Hate to see a woman having pleasure, particularly sexual pleasure. I mean, make a nice pair of soft cotton underwear with a French tickler built in. Women would be coming all day long, coming in the supermarket, coming on the subway, coming, happy vaginas. They wouldn't be able to stand it. Seeing all those energized, not-taking-shit, hot, happy vaginas.

If my vagina could talk, it would talk about itself like me; it would talk about other vaginas; it would do vagina impressions.

It would wear Harry Winston diamonds, no clothing—just there, all draped in diamonds.

My vagina helped release a giant baby. It thought it would be doing more of that. It's not. Now it wants to travel, doesn't want a lot of company. It wants to read and know things and get out more. It wants sex. It loves sex. It wants to go deeper. It's hungry for depth. It wants kindness. It wants change. It wants silence and freedom and gentle kisses and warm liquids and deep touch. It wants chocolate. It wants to scream. It wants to stop being angry. It wants to come. It wants to want. It wants. My vagina, my vagina. Well . . . it wants everything.

For the last ten years I have been actively involved with women who have no homes, women we call "homeless people" so we can categorize and forget them. I have done all kinds of things with these women, who have become my friends. I run recovery groups for women who have been raped or suffered incest, and groups for women addicted to drugs and alcohol. I go to the movies with these women, I have meals with them. I hang out. Over the past ten years I have interviewed hundreds of women. In all that time I have met only two who were not subjected to incest as young girls or raped as young women. I have evolved a theory that for most of these women, "home" is a very scary place, a place they have fled, and that the shelters where I meet them are the first places many of them ever find safety, protection, or comfort, in the community of other women.

This monologue is one woman's story as she told it to me. I met her about five years ago, in a shelter. I would like to tell you it's an unusual story—brutal; extreme. But it's not. In fact, it's not nearly as disturbing as many of the stories I've heard in the years since. Poor women suffer terrible sexual violence that goes unreported. Because of their social class, these women do not have access to therapy or other methods of healing. Their repeated abuse ultimately eats away at their self-esteem, driving them to drugs, prostitution, AIDS, and in many cases, death. Fortunately, this particular story has a different outcome. This woman met another woman in that shelter, and they fell in love. Through their love, they got out of the shelter system and have a beautiful life together today. I wrote this piece for them, for their amazing spirits, for the women we do not see, who hurt and who need us.

THE LITTLE COOCHI SNORCHER THAT COULD

[Southern woman of color]

Memory: December 1965; Five Years Old

My mama tells me in a scary, loud, life-threatening voice to stop scratching my coochi snorcher. I become terrified that I've scratched it off down there. I do not touch myself again, even in the bath. I am afraid of the water getting in and filling me up so I explode. I put Band-Aids over my coochi snorcher to cover the hole, but they fall off in the water. I imagine a stopper, a bathtub plug up there to prevent things from entering me. I sleep with three pairs of happy heart-patterned cotton underpants underneath my snap-up paja-mas. I still want to touch myself, but I don't.

Memory: Seven Years Old

Edgar Montane, who is ten, gets angry at me and punches me with all his might between my legs. It feels like he breaks my entire self. I limp home. I can't pee. My mama asks me what's wrong with my coochi snorcher, and when I tell her what Edgar did to me she yells at me and says never to let anyone touch me down there again. I try to explain he didn't touch it, Mama, he punched it.

Memory: Nine Years Old

I play on the bed, bouncing and falling, and impale my coochi snorcher on the bedpost. I make high-pitched screamy noises that come straight from my coochi snorcher's mouth. I get taken to the hospital and they sew it up down there from where it's been torn apart.

Memory: Ten Years Old

I'm at my father's house and he's having a party upstairs. Everyone's drinking. I'm playing alone in the basement and I'm trying on my new white cotton bra and panties that my father's girl-friend gave me. Suddenly my father's best friend, this big man Alfred, comes up from behind and pulls my new underpants down and sticks his big hard penis into my coochi scorcher. I scream. I kick. I try to fight him off, but he already gets it in.. My father's there then and he has a gun and there's a loud horrible noise and then there's blood all over Alfred and me, lots of blood. I'm sure my coochi snorcher is finally falling out. Al-fred is paralyzed for life and my mama doesn't let me see my father for seven years.

Memory: Thirteen Years Old

My coochi snorcher is a very bad place, a place of pain, nastiness, punching, invasion, and blood. It's a site for mishaps. It's a bad-luck zone. I imagine a freeway between my legs and, girl, I am traveling, going far away from here.

Memory: Sixteen Years Old

There's this gorgeous twenty-four-year-old woman in our neighborhood and I stare at her all the time. One day she invites me into her car. She asks me if I like to kiss boys, and I tell her I do not like that. Then she says she wants to show me something, and she leans over and kisses me so softly on the lips with her lips and then puts her tongue in my mouth. Wow. She asks me if I want to come over to her house, and then she kisses me again and tells me to relax, to feel it, to let our tongues feel it. She asks my mama if I can spend the night and my mother's delighted that such a beautiful, successful woman has taken an interest in me. I'm scared but really I can't wait. Her apartment's fantastic. She's got it hooked up. It's the seventies: the beads, the fluffy pillows, the mood lights. I decide right there that I want to be a secretary like her when I grow up. She makes a vodka for herself and then she asks what I want to drink. I say the same as she's drinking and she says she doesn't think my mama would like me drinking vodka. I say she probably wouldn't like me kissing girls, either, and the pretty lady makes me a drink. Then she changes into this chocolate satin teddy. She's so beautiful. I always thought bulldaggers were ugly. I say, "You look great," and she says, "So do you." I say, "But I only have this white cotton bra and underpants." Then she dresses me, slowly, in another satin teddy. It's lavender like the first soft days of spring. The alcohol has gone to my head and I'm loose and ready. I noticed that there's a picture over her bed of a naked black woman with a huge afro as she gently and slowly lays me out on the bed. And just our bodies rubbing makes me come. Then she does everything to me and my coochi snorcher that I always thought was nasty before, and wow. I'm so hot, so wild. She says, "Your vagina, untouched by man, smells so nice, so fresh, wish I could keep it that way forever." I get crazy wild and then the phone rings and of course it's my mama. I'm sure she knows; she catches me at everything. I'm breathing so heavy and I try to act normal when I get on the phone and she asks me, "What's wrong with you, have you been running?" I say, "No, Mama, exercising." Then she tells the beautiful secretary to make sure I'm not around boys and the lady tells her, "Trust me, there's no boys around here." Afterward the gorgeous lady teaches me everything about my coochi snorcher. She makes me play with myself in front of her and she teaches me all the different ways to give myself pleasure. She's very thorough. She tells me to always know how to give myself pleasure so I'll never need to rely on a man. In the morning I am worried that I've become a butch because I'm so in love with her. She laughs, but I never see her again. I realized later she was my surprising, unexpected, politically incorrect salvation. She transformed my sorry-ass coochi snorcher and raised it up into a kind of heaven.

During the course of my run in New York, I received this letter:

As the honorary chair of the Vulva Club, we would be more than pleased to make you a member. However, when Harriet Lerner developed this club over twenty years ago, membership was predicated on the understanding and correct usage of the word *vulva* and being able to communicate that to as many people as possible, especially women.

Warm regards,

Jane Hirschman

THE VULVA CLUB

I have always been obsessed with naming things. If I could name them, I could know them. If I could name them, I could tame them. They could be my friends.

For example, I had a large collection of frogs when I was a little girl: stuffed frogs, china frogs, plastic frogs, neon frogs, happy battery-operated frogs. Each one had a name. I took time to know them for a while before I named them. I sat them on my bed and would watch them in daylight, wear them in my coat pocket, hold them in my sweaty little hands. I came to know them by their texture, their smell, their shape, their size, their sense of humor. Then they would get named, usually in a splendid naming ceremony. Surrounding them with their frog friends, I would dress them in ceremonial coats, put sparkles on them, or gold stars, stand them in front of the frog chapel, and name them.

First, I would whisper the coveted name into their ear. *(whispering)* "You are my Froggie Doodle Mashy Pie." I would make sure the frog accepted the name. Then I would say it out loud for the other excited frogs, some of whom were waiting for their own names. "Froggie Doodle Mashy Pie." Then there would be singing, usually the name repeated over and over, joined by the other frogs. *(make up a song)* "Froggie Doodle Mashy Pie. Froggie Doodle Mashy Pie." This would happen with dancing.

I would line the froggies up and dance in and out of them, hopping like a frog and making general frog noises, always holding the newly christened frog in my hands or arms, depending on the size. It was an exhausting ceremony, but crucial. It would have been fine if it had been limited to frogs, but soon I needed to name everything. I named rugs and doors and chairs and stairs. Ben, for example, was my flashlight, named after my kindergarten teacher, who was always in my business.

I eventually named all the parts of my body. My hands—Gladys. They seemed functional and basic, like Gladys. I named my shoulders Shorty—strong and a little belligerent. My breasts were Betty. They weren't Veronica, but they weren't ugly either. Naming my "down there" was not so easy. It wasn't the same as naming my hands. No, it was complicated. Down there was alive, not so easy to pinpoint. It remained unnamed and, as unnamed, it was untamed, unknown.

We had a baby-sitter around then, Sara Stanley. She talked in this high-pitched voice that made me pee. When I was taking a bath one night, she told me to be sure to wash my "Itsy Bitsy." I can't say that I liked this name. It took a while even to figure out what it was. But there was something about her voice. The name stuck. Yes, there it is, my Itsy Bitsy.

Unfortunately, this name followed me into adulthood. On our first night in bed, I informed the man I would later marry that Itsy Bitsy was a little shy but eager, and if he would be patient, she would surely reveal her mysteries. He was a bit freaked out, I think, but as is his nature, he went along with it and later would actually call her by name. "Is Itsy Bitsy there? Is she ready?" I myself was never happy with her name, and so what happened later is not really surprising.

One night, my husband and I were in the act. He called out to her, "Come here, my little Itsy Bitsy," and she did not respond. It was as if she suddenly wasn't there. "Itsy Bitsy, it's me, your biggest fan." No word. No motion. So I called to her.

"Itsy Bitsy, come on out. Don't do this to me."

Not a word, not a sound. Itsy was dead and mute and gone.

"Itsy Bitsy!"

For days she did not come, then weeks, then months. I became despondent.

I reluctantly told my friend Teresa, who was spending all her time in this new women's group. I said, "Itsy Bitsy will not speak to me, Teresa. She won't return my calls."

"Who is Itsy Bitsy?"

"My Bitsy," I said. "My Itsy."

"What are you talking about?" she said in a voice that suddenly sounded much deeper than mine. "You mean your vulva, girl?"

"Vulva," I said to Teresa. "What exactly is that?"

"It's the package," she said. "It's the entire deal."

Vulva. Vulva. I could feel something unlock. Itsy Bitsy was wrong. I knew this all along. I could not see Itsy Bitsy. I never knew who or what she was, and she did not sound like an opening or a lip.

That night, we named her—my husband, Randy, and I. Just like the frogs. Dressed her in sparkles and sexy clothes, put her in front of the body chapel, lit candles. At first we whispered it, "Vulva, vulva," softly to see if she'd hear. "Vulva, vulva, are you there?" There was sweetness and something definitely stirred. "Vulva, vulva, are you real?"

And we sang the vulva song, which didn't involve croaking but kissing, and we danced the vulva dance, which didn't involve hopping but leaping, and all the other body parts were lined up—Betty and Gladys and Shorty—and they were definitely listening.

In some places, Africans seem to have been quietly putting an end to the tradition of genital cutting. In Guinea, for instance, Aja Tounkara Diallo Fatimata, the chief "cutter" in the capital, Conakry, used to be reviled by Western human-rights groups. Then a few years ago, she confessed that she had never actually cut anybody. "I'd just cinch their clitorises to make them scream," she said, "and tightly bandage them up so that they walked as though they were in pain."

—from the Center for Reproductive Law and Policy

"What does a vagina smell like?"

Earth.

Wet garbage.

God.

Water.

A brand-new morning.

Depth.

Sweet ginger.

Sweat.

Depends.

Musk.

Me.

No smell, I've been told.

Pineapple.

Chalice essence.

Paloma Picasso.

Earthy meat and musk.

Cinnamon and cloves.

Roses.

Spicy musky jasmine forest, deep, deep forest.

Damp moss.

Yummy candy.

The South Pacific.

Somewhere between fish and lilacs.

Peaches.

The woods.

Ripe fruit.

Strawberry-kiwi tea.

Fish.

Heaven.

Vinegar and water.

Light, sweet liquor.

Cheese.

Ocean.

Sexy.

A sponge.

The beginning.

I have been traveling with this piece all over America (and now, the world) for years. I am threatening to create a vagina-friendly map of all the vagina-friendly cities I have visited. There are many now. There have been many surprises; Oklahoma City surprised me. They were wild for vaginas in Oklahoma City. Pittsburgh surprised me. They love vaginas in Pittsburgh. I have already been there three times. Wherever I go, women come up to me after the show to tell me their sto-

ries, to make suggestions, to communicate their re-
sponses. This is my favorite part of traveling with the
work. I get to hear the truly amazing stories. They are
told so simply, so matter-of-factly. I am always re-
minded how extraordinary women's lives are, and how
profound. And I am reminded how isolated women are,
and how oppressed they often become in their isolation.
How few people they have ever told of their suffering and
confusion. How much shame there is surrounding all
this. How crucial it is for women to tell their stories, to
share them with other people, how our survival as
women depends on this dialogue.

It was after performing the piece one night in New
York City that I heard the story of a young Vietnamese
woman who, when she was five years old—recently ar-
rived in America, unable to speak English—fell on a fire
hydrant while playing with her best friend, and cut her
vagina. Unable to communicate what had occurred, she
simply hid her bloodied underpants under her bed. Her
mother found them and assumed she'd been raped. As
the young girl did not know the word for "fire hydrant,"
she could not explain to her parents what had really

happened. Her parents accused her best friend's brother of raping her. They rushed the young girl to the hospital, and a whole group of men stood around her bed, staring at her open, exposed vagina. Then, on the way home, she realized her father was no longer looking at her. In his eyes she had become a used, finished woman. He never really looked at her again.

Or the story of the stunning young woman in Oklahoma, who approached me after the show with her stepmother to tell me how she had been born without a vagina, and only realized it when she was fourteen. She was playing with her girlfriend. They compared their genitals and she realized hers were different, something was wrong. She went to the gynecologist with her father, the parent she was close to, and the doctor discovered that in fact she did not have a vagina or a uterus. Her father was heartbroken, trying to repress his tears and sadness so his daughter would not feel bad. On the way home from the doctor, in a noble attempt to comfort her, he said, "Don't worry, darlin'. This is all gonna be just fine. As a matter of fact, it's gonna be great. We're gonna get you the best homemade pussy in America.

And when you meet your husband, he's gonna know we had it made specially for him." And they did get her a new pussy, and she was relaxed and happy and when she brought her father back two nights later, the love between them melted me.

Then there was the night in Pittsburgh when a woman filled with passion rushed up to tell me she had to speak to me as soon as possible. Her intensity convinced me, and I called her as soon as I got back to New York. She said she was a massage therapist and she had to talk to me about the texture of the vagina. The texture was crucial. I hadn't gotten the texture, she said. And she talked to me for an hour with such detail, with such sensuous clarity, that when she was finished, I had to lie down. During that conversation she also talked to me about the word "cunt." I had said something negative about it in my performance, and she said I didn't understand the word at all. She needed to help me reconceive it. She talked to me for a half-hour more about the word "cunt" and when she was finished, I was a convert. I wrote this for her.

RECLAIMING CUNT

I call it cunt. I've reclaimed it, "cunt." I really like it. "Cunt." Listen to it. "Cunt." C C, Ca Ca. Cavern, cackle, clit, cute, come—closed c—closed inside, inside ca—then u—then cu—then curvy, inviting sharkskin u—uniform, under, up, urge, ugh, ugh, u—then n then cun—snug letters fitting perfectly together—n—nest, now, nexus, nice, nice, always depth, always round in uppercase, cun, cun—n a jagged wicked electrical pulse—

n [high-pitched noise] then soft n—warm n—cun, cun, then t—then sharp certain tangy t—texture, take, tent, tight, tantalizing, tensing, taste, tendrils, time, tactile, tell me, tell me "Cunt cunt," say it, tell me "Cunt." "Cunt."

I ASKED A SIX-YEAR-OLD GIRL:

"If your vagina got dressed, what would it wear?"

"Red high-tops and a Mets cap worn backward."

"If it could speak, what would it say?"

"It would say words that begin with 'V' and 'T'—'turtle' and 'violin' are examples."

"What does your vagina remind you of?"

"A pretty dark peach. Or a diamond I found from a treasure and it's mine."

"What's special about your vagina?"

"Somewhere deep inside it I know it has a re-ally really smart brain."

"What does your vagina smell like?"

"Snowflakes."

THE WOMAN
WHO LOVED TO MAKE
VAGINAS HAPPY

I love vaginas. I love women. I do not see them as separate things. Women pay me to dominate them, to excite them, to make them come. I did not start out like this. No, to the contrary: I started out as a lawyer. But in my late thirties, I became obsessed with making women happy. There were so many unfulfilled women. So many women who had no access to their sexual happiness. It began as a mission of sorts, but then I got involved in it. I got very good at it, kind of brilliant. It was my art. I started getting paid for it. It was as if I had found my calling. Tax law seemed completely boring and insignificant then.

I wore outrageous outfits when I dominated women—lace and silk and leather—and I used props: whips, handcuffs, rope, dildos. There was nothing like this in tax law. There were no props, no excitement, and I hated those blue corporate suits, although I wear them now from time to time in my new line of work and they serve quite nicely. Context is all. There were no props, no outfits in corporate law. There was no wetness. There was no dark mysterious foreplay. There were no erect nipples. There were no delicious mouths, but mainly there was no moaning. Not the kind I'm talking about, anyway. This was the key, I see now; moaning was the thing that ultimately seduced me and got me addicted to making women happy. When I was a little girl and I would see women in the movies making love, making strange orgasmic moaning noises, I used to laugh.

I got strangely hysterical. I couldn't believe that big, outrageous, ungoverned sounds like that just came out of women.

I longed to moan. I practiced in front of my mirror, on a tape recorder, moaning in various keys, various tones, with sometimes very operatic expressions, sometimes with more reserved, almost withheld expression. But always when I played it back, it sounded fake. It *was* fake. It wasn't rooted in anything sexual, really, only in my desire to be sexual.

But then when I was ten I had to pee really badly once. On a car trip. It went on for almost an hour and when I finally got to pee in this dirty little gas station, it was so exciting, I moaned. I moaned as I peed. I couldn't believe it, me moaning in a Texaco station somewhere in the middle of Louisiana. I realized right then that moans are connected with not getting what you want right away, with putting things off. I realized moans were best when they caught you by surprise; they came out of this hidden mysterious part of you that was speaking its own language. I realized that moans were, in fact, that language.

I became a moaner. It made most men anxious. Frankly, it terrified them. I was loud and they couldn't concentrate on what they were doing. They'd lose focus. Then they'd lose everything. We couldn't make love in people's homes. The walls were too thin. I got a reputation in my building, and people stared at me with contempt in the elevator. Men thought I was too intense; some called me insane.

I began to feel bad about moaning. I got quiet and polite. I made noise into a pillow. I learned to choke my moan, hold it back like a sneeze. I began to get headaches and stress-related disorders. I was becoming hopeless when I discovered women. I discovered that most women loved my moaning—but, more important, I discovered how deeply excited I got when other women moaned, when I could make other women moan. It became a kind of passion.

Discovering the key, unlocking the vagina's mouth, unlocking this voice, this wild song.

I made love to quiet women and I found this place inside them and they shocked themselves in their moaning. I made love to moaners and they found a deeper, more penetrating moan. I became obsessed. I longed to make women moan, to be in charge, like a conductor, maybe, or a bandleader.

It was a kind of surgery, a kind of delicate science, finding the tempo, the exact location or home of the moan. That's what I called it.

Sometimes I found it over a woman's jeans. Sometimes I sneaked up on it, off the record, quietly disarming the surrounding alarms and moving in. Sometimes I used force, but not violent, oppressing force, more like dominating, "I'm going to take you someplace; don't worry, lie back, enjoy the ride" kind of force. Sometimes it was simply mundane. I found the moan before things even started, while we were eating salad or chicken just casually right there, with my fingers,

"Here it is like that," real simple, in the kitchen, all mixed in with the balsamic vinegar. Sometimes I used props—I loved props—sometimes I made the woman find her own moan in front of me. I waited, stuck it out until she opened herself. I wasn't fooled by the minor, more obvious moans. No, I pushed her further, all the way into her power moan.

There's the clit moan (a soft, in-the-mouth sound), the vaginal moan (a deep, in-the-throat sound), the combo clit-vaginal moan. There's the pre-moan (a hint of sound), the almost moan (a circling sound), the right-on-it moan (a deeper, definite sound), the elegant moan (a sophisticated laughing sound), the Grace Slick moan (a rock-singing sound), the WASP moan (no sound), the semireligious moan (a Muslim chanting sound), the mountaintop moan (a yodeling sound), the baby moan (a googie-googie-googie-goo sound), the doggy moan (a panting sound), the southern moan (southern accent—"yeah! yeah"), the uninhibited militant bisexual moan (a deep, aggressive, pounding sound), the machine-gun moan, the tortured Zen moan (a twisted, hungry sound), the diva moan (a high, operatic note), the twisted-toe-orgasm moan, and, finally, the surprise triple orgasm moan.

After I finished this piece I read it to the woman on whose interview I'd based it. She didn't feel it really had anything to do with her. She loved the piece, mind you, but she didn't see herself in it. She felt that I had somehow avoided talking about vaginas, that I was still somehow objectifying them. Even the moans were a way of objectifying the vagina, cutting it off from the rest of the vagina, the rest of the woman. There was a real dif-

ference in the way lesbians saw vaginas. I hadn't yet captured it.

So I interviewed her again.

"As a lesbian," she said, "I need you to start from a lesbian-centered place, not framed within a heterosexual context. I did not desire women, for example, because I disliked men. Men weren't even part of the equation." She said, "You need to talk about entering into vaginas. You can't talk about lesbian sex without doing this.

"For example," she said. "I'm having sex with a woman. She's inside me. I'm inside me. Fucking myself together with her. There are four fingers inside me; two are hers, two are mine."

I don't know that I wanted to talk about sex. But then again, how can I talk about vaginas without talking about them in action? I am worried about the titillation factor, worried about the piece becoming exploitative. Am I talking about vaginas to arouse people? Is that a bad thing?

"As lesbians," she said, *"we know about vaginas. We touch them. We lick them. We play with them. We tease them. We notice when the clitoris swells. We notice our own."*

I realize I am embarrassed, listening to her. There is a combination of reasons: excitement, fear, her love of vaginas and comfort with them and my distancing, terror of saying all this in front of you, the audience.

"I like to play with the rim of the vagina," she said, *"with fingers, knuckles, toes, tongue. I like to enter it slowly, slowly entering, then thrusting three fingers inside.*

"There's other cavities, other openings; there's the mouth. While I have a free hand, there's fingers in her mouth, fingers in her vagina, both going, all going all at

once, her mouth sucking my fingers, her vagina sucking my fingers. Both sucking, both wet."

I realize I don't know what is appropriate. I don't even know what that word means. Who decides. I learn so much from what she's telling me. About her, about me.

"Then I come to my own wetness," she says. "She can enter me. I can experience my own wetness, let her slide her fingers into me, her fingers into my mouth, my vagina, the same. I pull her hand out of my cunt. I rub my wetness against her knee so she knows. I slide my wetness down her leg until my face is between her thighs."

Does talking about vaginas ruin the mystery, or is that just another myth that keeps vaginas in the dark, keeps them unknowing and unsatisfied?

"My tongue is on her clitoris. My tongue replaces my fingers. My mouth enters her vagina."

Saying these words feels naughty, dangerous, too direct, too specific, wrong, intense, in charge, alive.

"My tongue is on her clitoris. My tongue replaces my fingers. My mouth enters her vagina."

To love women, to love our vaginas, to know them and touch them and be familiar with who we are and what we need. To satisfy ourselves, to teach our lovers to satisfy us, to be present in our vaginas, to speak of them out loud, to speak of their hunger and pain and loneliness and humor, to make them visible so they cannot be ravaged in the dark without great consequence, so that our center, our point, our motor, our dream, is no longer detached, mutilated, numb, broken, invisible, or ashamed.

"You have to talk about entering vaginas," she said. "Come on," I say, "come in."

I had been performing this piece for over two years when it suddenly occurred to me that there were no pieces about birth. It was a bizarre omission. Although when I told a journalist this recently, he asked me, "What's the connection?"

Almost twenty-one years ago I adopted a son, Dylan, who was very close in age to me. Last year he and his wife, Shiva, had a baby. They asked me to be present for the birth. I don't think, in all my investiga-

tion, that I really understood vaginas until this mo-ment. If I was in awe of them before the birth of my granddaughter, Colette, I am certainly in deep worship now.

I WAS THERE IN
THE ROOM

For Shiva

I was there when her vagina opened.
We were all there: her mother, her husband,
    and I,
and the nurse from the Ukraine with her
    whole hand
up there in her vagina feeling and turning with
    her rubber
glove as she talked casually to us—like she was
    turning on a loaded faucet.

I was there in the room when the contractions
made her crawl on all fours,
made unfamiliar moans leak out of her pores
and still there after hours when she just
        screamed suddenly
wild, her arms striking at the electric air.

I was there when her vagina changed
from a shy sexual hole
to an archaeological tunnel, a sacred vessel,
a Venetian canal, a deep well with a tiny stuck
        child inside,
waiting to be rescued.

I saw the colors of her vagina. They changed.
Saw the bruised broken blue
the blistering tomato red
the gray pink, the dark;
saw the blood like perspiration along the edges
saw the yellow, white liquid, the shit, the clots
pushing out all the holes, pushing harder and
        harder,

saw through the hole, the baby's head
scratches of black hair, saw it just there behind
the bone—a hard round memory,
as the nurse from the Ukraine kept turning and
    turning
her slippery hand.

I was there when each of us, her mother and I,
held a leg and spread her wide pushing
with all our strength against her pushing
and her husband sternly counting, "One, two,
    three,"
telling her to focus, harder.
We looked into her then.
We couldn't get our eyes out of that place.

We forget the vagina, all of us
what else would explain
our lack of awe, our lack of wonder.

I was there when the doctor
reached in with Alice in Wonderland spoons

and there as her vagina became a wide operatic
     mouth
singing with all its strength;
first the little head, then the gray flopping arm,
     then the fast
swimming body, swimming quickly into our
     weeping arms.

I was there later when I just turned and faced
     her vagina.
I stood and let myself see
her all spread, completely exposed
mutilated, swollen, and torn,
bleeding all over the doctor's hands
who was calmly sewing her there.

I stood, and as I stared, her vagina suddenly
became a wide red pulsing heart.

The heart is capable of sacrifice.
So is the vagina.
The heart is able to forgive and repair.

It can change its shape to let us in.

It can expand to let us out.

So can the vagina.

It can ache for us and stretch for us, die for us

and bleed and bleed us into this difficult,

    wondrous world.

So can the vagina.

I was there in the room.

I remember.

SPOTLIGHT MONOLOGUES

Each of these monologues was written for a V-Day Spotlight or a situation in the world where women were totally at risk, where they had been raped or murdered or dismissed or simply not allowed to be. It is my hope that in the telling of these stories where women suffered, they will be healed, in seeing what erased them, they will be made forever visible, honored, and protected.

THE MEMORY
OF HER FACE

For Esther

Islamabad

They all knew something terrible

Was going to happen

Each time he came home

The things he used

First time

He grabbed the closest thing

He grabbed a pot

He smashed her head

He smashed her right eye hard

The next time

He thought about it a little

And paused

Took off his belt

She had gashes inside her thighs

The third time he needed to be more

Involved in hurting her

So he beat her with his fists

He broke her nose

They heard her screams

They heard her beg

They didn't, wouldn't intervene

She was his

Unwritten law.

Don't ask what she had done

It was just her face that pissed him off

Just her needy face waiting for more

The last time he

Had enough of her

He planned it out

He got the acid in advance

He poured it in a jar

She said she needed money for food for them

She looked like that.
Like that. Like that. Like that.
Her face is gone
Totally melted off
Just eyes that's all you see
That's all
Just eyes encased in gooey flesh
I tell you this because
She's there inside this mess
Inside this monstrous mask
Inside the death of her esteem
Inside his wish to make her none
She's there, I swear
I heard her wheeze
I heard her sigh
I heard her babble something
With what was once her mouth
I heard her. I swear
She lives in there.

Juárez

Each woman is dark, particular, young
Each woman has brown eyes

Each woman is gone

There is one girl missing for ten months

She was seventeen when they took her away

She worked in the maquiladora

She stamped thousands of coupons of products

She would never afford

Four dollars a day

They paid her and bused her to the desert

To sleep in freezing shit

It must have been on the way to the bus

They took her

It must have been dark outside

It must have lasted until morning

Whatever they did to her

It went on and on

You can tell from the others

Who showed up without hands or nipples

It must have gone on and on.

When she finally reappeared

She was bone

Bone bone

No cute mole above her right eye

No naughty smile, no wavy black hair
Bone she came back as bone
She and the others
All beautiful
All beginning
All coupons
All faces
All gone
300 faces gone
300 noses
300 chins
300 dark penetrating eyes
300 smiles
300 mulatto cheeks
300 hungry mouths
about to speak
about to tell
about to scream
gone now bone.

I tried to turn away
When she lifted her chador

in the restaurant

When they raised the plastic cloth

that concealed

the bone outline of her head

in the morgue

I tried to turn away.

UNDER THE BURQA

For Zoya

(This piece is not about the burqa per se. Wearing one is obviously a matter of culture and choice. The piece is about a time and place where women had no choice.)

imagine a huge dark piece of cloth
hung over your entire body
like you were a shameful statue
imagine there's only a drop of light
enough to know there is still daylight for others
imagine it's hot, very hot
imagine you are being encased in cloth,

drowning in fabric, in darkness

imagine you are begging in this bedspread

reaching out your hand inside the cloth

which must remained covered, unpolished,

     unseen

or they might smash it or cut it off

imagine no one is putting rubies in your

     invisible hand

because no one can see your face

so you do not exist

imagine you cannot find your children

because they came for your husband

the only man you ever loved

even though it was an arranged marriage

because they came and shot him with the gun

of his they could not find

and you tried to defend him and they trampled

     you

four men on your back

in front of your screaming children

imagine you went mad

but you did not know you were mad

because you were living under a bedspread
and you hadn't seen the sun in years
and you lost your way
and you remembered your two daughters
    vaguely
like a dream the way you remembered sky
imagine muttering as a way of talking
because words did not form anymore in the
    darkness
and you did not cry because it got too hot and
    wet in there
imagine bearded men that you could only
    decipher
by their smell
checking your socks and beating you
because they were white
imagine being flogged
in front of people you could not see
imagine being humiliated so deeply
that there was no face attached to it
and no air. it got darker there
imagine no peripheral vision

so like a wounded animal

you could not defend yourself

or even duck from the sideward blows

imagine that laughter was banned

throughout your country and music

and the only sounds you heard

were the muffled sounds of the azun

or the cries of other women flogged

inside their cloth, inside their dark

imagine you could no longer distinguish

between living and dying

so you stopped trying to kill yourself

because it would be redundant

imagine you had no place to live

your roof was the cloth

as you wandered the streets

and this tomb

was getting smaller and smellier every day

you were beginning to walk into things

imagine suffocating while you were still

     breathing

imagine muttering and screaming

inside a cage

and no one is hearing

imagine me inside the inside

of the darkness in you

i am caught there

i am lost there

inside the cloth

which is your head

inside the dark we share

imagine you can see me

i was beautiful once

big dark eyes

you would know me

THEY BEAT THE GIRL OUT OF MY BOY . . . OR SO THEY TRIED

For Calpernia and Andrea

At five years old
I was putting my baby sister's
diapers on
I saw her vagina
I wanted one
I wanted one
I thought it would grow
I thought I would open
I ached to belong

I ached to smell

like my mother

Her aroma lived in my hair

on my hands, in my skin

I ached to be pretty

Pretty

I wondered why I was missing my

bathing suit top at the beach

Why I wasn't dressed like the other girls

I ached to be completed

I ached to belong

To play the baton

They assigned me a sex

The day I was born

It's as random as being adopted

or being assigned a hotel room on the thirtieth
      floor

It has nothing to do with who you are

or your fear of heights.

But in spite of the apparatus

I was forced to carry around

I always knew I was a girl

They beat me for it

They beat me for crying

They pummeled me for wanting

To touch

To pet

To hug

To help

To hold

Their hands

For trying to fly in church

like Sister Bertrille

For doing cartwheels

Crocheting socks

For carrying purses to kindergarten

They kicked the shit out of me every day

on my way to school.

In the park

they smashed my

Magic Marker painted nails

They punched my lipsticked mouth

They beat the girl

out of my boy

or they tried

So I went underground

I stopped playing the flute

"Be a man, stand up for yourself

Go punch him back."

I grew a full beard

It was good I was big

I joined the Marines

"Suck it up and drive on."

I became duller

Jaded

Sometimes cruel

Butch it

Butch it

Butch it up

Always clenched, inaccurate,

Incomplete

I ran away from home

from school

from boot camp.

Ran to Miami

Greenwich Village

The Aleutian Islands

New Orleans

I found gay people

Wilderness lesbians

Got my first hormone shot

Got permission to be myself

To transition

To travel

To immigrate

350 hours of hot needles

I would count the male particles as they died

Sixteen man hairs gone

The feminine is in your face

I lift my eyebrows more

I'm curious

I ask questions.

And my voice

Practice practice

It's all about resonance

Sing song sing song

Men are monotone and flat

Southern accents are really excellent

Jewish accents really help.

"Hello my friend"

And my vagina is so much friendlier

I cherish it

It brings me joy

The orgasms come in waves

Before they were jerky

I'm the girl next door

My Lieutenant Colonel father ended

up paying for it

My vagina

My mother was worried

what people would think

of her, that she made this happen

until I came to church

and everyone said you have a beautiful

daughter

I wanted to belong

I got to be soft

I am allowed to listen

I am allowed to touch

I am able to receive.

To be in the present tense

People are so much nicer to me now

I can wake up in the morning

Put my hair in a ponytail

A wrong was righted

I am right with God

It's like when you're trying to sleep

And there is a loud car alarm

When I got my vagina, it was like someone

Finally turned it off

I live now in the female zone

But you know how people feel about immigrants

They don't like it when you come from

    someplace else

They don't like it when you mix

They killed my boyfriend

They beat him insanely as he slept

With a baseball bat

They beat this girl

Out of his head

They didn't want him

Dating a foreigner

Even though she was pretty

And she listened and was kind

They didn't want him falling in love

with ambiguity.

They were that terrified of love.

(This piece was based on interviews with Transwomen from all over America.)

CROOKED BRAID

For the women from the Oglala Lakota Nation

1

He wanted to go out.

He said to me "You stay home"

I said "I wanted to go out"

He said "You have a baby"

I said "It's our baby"

I laid the baby down.

He probably felt my tension

because he was whimpering,

the baby.

I looked up

and he slapped me, my husband.

Not a blast that knocks your eyes blue.

That came later.

It was a smack,

a hard domestic smack.

He looked at me.

He was smiling.

I couldn't believe it.

He was smiling.

He slapped me again.

His dad was vicious to his mother.

I saw him smile.

What was that?

He was the nicest person.

Hc had long black hair.

When we made love it got

loose

before.

2

He took me to the dinner,

made me go out with his boss.

I didn't want to go.

He kicked me under the table,

told me to look happy,

told me to smile.

I smiled.

He kicked me again,

asked me who I was trying to

fuck, told me to stop coming

on to everyone.

I stopped smiling.

He kicked me again.

This went on and on.

Outside the restaurant

he grabbed my hair

and pulled me down to

the curb.

It had been snowing.

He buried me in snow.

He pounded me in the gutter.

The snow was melting.

It was sloppy.

My hair felt like it was bleeding.

3

He was drinking.

I was too.

I must have blacked out.

I woke up in the hospital

after five brain surgeries.

My hair was gone.

They shaved it off.

I had to relearn to talk

and move my arms.

It took me four months

to remember how to cook

breakfast.

I remember putting

the egg in the frying pan

with the bacon.

I knew the egg felt right

I just didn't remember to

crack it open.

Just the egg in the frying pan

in its shell.

My head was bald.

4

Eighteen years

he beat me.

In the morning

when he was so nice again

I would braid his long hair.

I would take my time

like I cared so much

and I would do it perfectly crooked.

I would make the hairs

so they would stand up

all crazy like.

Then he'd go forgetting

that the bruises on my

face were his handprints.

He'd walk all cocky in the street.

All macho in the road,

but his braid would be so crooked

and look so stupid and wrong.

This shouldn't have made me that happy.

It really just shouldn't have made me that

    happy.

5

Heard that he was out

with a woman

making love and she was fluffing

his hair when he was wild

on top of her.

He came home

much later

and his hair was braided up all

right and tight.

He passed out

from drinking.

Then I got up

with scissors

as he snored

and slowly walked to him

and just cut the braid off,

completely off,

and put it in his hand

so that when he woke

up he screamed

"What the

fuck? I am going to kill you"

and he jumped up,

but I had tied his shoes together

so he couldn't run.

I didn't go

back to him for three years

until I knew his hair had grown out again.

6

I didn't want to have sex with him.

He was drunk.

I was just a piece of meat

to him,

a hole.

I tried to pretend

I was asleep.

He elbowed me, jerked me

pulled me up.

I remember thinking just get it over with.

He was soft and kept pumping

and pumping until

I got sore.

I said "It didn't feel good."

He said "Who were you with?

Was he bigger than

me? Did you like it?"

You're like a mouse with a lion.

You have to move fast

to the door.

He picked me up

like I was a rag.

His eyes were numb.

I could hear my son screaming,

his mouth was open and

his tonsils,

I could see his tonsils.

My husband beat the shit out of me.

He wrapped my long black hair around his
        hand,

jerked my head.

I tried to get my son.

"That's not your son," he said,

holding my hair in his hand.

"That's not your son anymore."

Now he calls me the middle

of night

weeping.

He didn't mean to beat his wife.

He didn't mean to batter her.

He's suicidal.

He knows what his mother went through.

But he can't stop—my son.

They took our land.

They took our ways.

They took our men.

We want them back.

(This piece was based on interviews with Native women on the Pine Ridge Reservation.)

S A Y   I T

For the "Comfort Women"

Our stories only exist inside our heads

Inside our ravaged bodies

Inside a time and space of war

And emptiness

There is no paper trail

Nothing official on the books

Only conscience

Only this

What we were promised:

That I would save my father if I went with

    them

That I would find a job

That I would serve the country

That they would kill me if I didn't go

That it was better there

What we found:

No mountains

No trees

No water

Yellow sand

A desert

A warehouse full of tears

Thousands of worried girls

My braid cut against my will

No time to wear panties

What we were forced to do:

Change our names

Wear one-piece dresses with

A button that opened easily

Fifty Japanese soldiers a day

Sometimes there would be a ship of them

Strange barbaric things

Do it even when we bleed

Do it young before we started bleeding

There were so many

Some wouldn't take off their clothes

Just took out their penis

So many men I couldn't walk

I couldn't stretch my legs

I couldn't bend

I couldn't

What they did to us over and over:

Cursed

Spanked

Twisted

Tore bloody inside out

Sterilized

Drugged

Slapped

Punched

What we saw:

A girl drinking chemicals in the bathroom

A girl killed by a bomb

A girl beaten with a rifle over and over

A girl running headfirst into a wall

A girl's malnourished body dumped in the river

To drown

What we weren't allowed to do:

Wash ourselves

Move around

Go to the doctor

Use a condom

Run away

Keep my baby

Ask him to stop

What we caught:

Malaria

Syphilis

Gonorrhea

Stillbirths

Tuberculosis

Heart disease

Nervous breakdowns

Hypochondria

What we were fed:

Rice

Miso soup

Turnip pickle

Rice

Miso soup

Turnip pickle

Rice rice rice

What we became:

Ruined

Tools

Infertile

Holes

Bloody

Meat

Exiled

Silenced

Alone

What we were left with:

Nothing

A shocked father who never recovered

And died

No wages

Scars

Hatred of Men

No children

No house

A space where a uterus once was

Booze

Smoking

Guilt

Shame

What we got called:

Ianfu—Comfort Women

Shugyofu—Women of Indecent Occupation

What we felt:

My chest still trembles

What got taken:

The springtime

My life

What we are:

74

79

84

93

Blind

Slow

Ready

Outside the Japanese Embassy every Wednesday

No longer afraid

What we want:

Now soon

Before we're gone

And our stories leave this world,

Leave our heads

Japanese government

Say it

Please

We are sorry, Comfort Women

Say it to me

We are sorry to me

We are sorry to me

To me

To me

To me

Say it.

Say sorry

Say we are sorry

Say me

See me

Say it

Sorry.

(This piece was based on the testimonies of the
Comfort Women.)

V - D A Y

v 10

V-DAY: TEN YEARS OF CHANGING

THE STORY OF WOMEN

Susan Celia Swan and Cecile Lipworth, Managing Directors, V-Day
Purva Panday, Programs and Campaigns Manager, V-Day

Spreading the Word

One out of every three women in the world today will experience physical or sexual violence in her lifetime. Usually this violence is inflicted by someone the woman knows—a relative, a neighbor, an adult in a position of authority. But political instability and armed conflict, fueled by religious, ethnic, and economic forces, threaten to further escalate the risk of such violence, because rape, battery, and sexual slavery have become increasingly used as weapons of war.

Although the sources of violence are diverse, women who have survived violence in any context describe tragically similar responses. Besides the pain and strength apparent in their stories of survival, the same themes resound across cultures and geographies: the indifference of authorities, the familial instinct of denial and secrecy, the lack of public outrage about the violence that millions of women experience each and every day.

Founded in 1998, V-Day is a global movement of grassroots activists dedicated to stopping every kind of violence against women and girls, including battery, rape, incest, female genital mutilation, and sexual slavery. V-Day activists believe that whole communities must name these violations as the crimes they are if the violence is to stop. V-Day's activities are designed to attack the silence—public and private—that allows violence against women to continue. Our work is grounded in three core beliefs: that art has the power to transform thinking and inspire people to act; that lasting social and cultural change is spread by ordinary people doing extraordinary things; and that local women know what their communities need and can become unstoppable leaders. V-Day is a catalyst, a torch for change. The *V* in V-Day stands for *Victory, Valentine,* and *Vagina.*

V-Day provides a path to action through benefit

productions of Eve Ensler's award-winning play *The Vagina Monologues*. With creativity, joy, reverence, and vision, V-Day activists around the world increase awareness and raise money to stop violence against women and girls in their own communities and globally. V-Day events have taken place in all 50 United States and in more than 119 countries. Since 1998, thousands of V-Day benefit performances have been produced by volunteer activists in the U.S. and around the world.

Performance is just the beginning. V-Day stages large-scale benefits and produces groundbreaking gatherings, films, and campaigns to educate and help change social attitudes toward violence against women. In ten years, the V-Day movement, a 501(c)(3) nonprofit, has raised $50 million and educated millions about the issue of violence against women and the efforts to end it; crafted international media, educational, and PSA campaigns; launched the Karama Program in the Middle East; reopened shelters; and funded more than five thousand community-based antiviolence programs and safe houses in Kenya, South Dakota, Egypt, Iraq, Haiti, and the Democratic Republic of the Congo.

Today, V-Day is housed in people's hearts and minds rather than in one physical location. Remarkably, a small group of eight paid staff—the V-Core—

work remotely from home bases around the world to sustain an infrastructure that keeps the V-Day network of millions of activists linked, informed, and engaged across the globe. V-Day is thus able to keep overhead costs amazingly low, enabling it to give away ninety-four cents of every dollar raised. A V-Board, made up of extraordinary women from the entertainment, business, and private sectors, along with a small group of tireless and longtime volunteers—the Vulva Choir—provide critical assistance and their many talents to V-Day's efforts. Eve Ensler, V-Day's founder and artistic Director, is a volunteer and has never received payment from V-Day for her work.

V-Day stands as a unique model of transformation and hope for millions. Through V-Day's empowerment philanthropy, women and men are provided with the tools to end violence in their own communities and to unearth the most promising solutions to keep women and girls safe. In ten short years, V-Day has achieved many hard-earned victories, building an international community of advocates for peace and justice and making a deep, lasting impact around the world. It has unraveled fixed ideas, illuminating how what was once acceptable is no longer conscionable. *V-Day is a reminder that the fight to end violence is not over.* By liberating rather than condemning, V-Day has become a vehicle to recovery and transformation, a movement that is changing the culture of violence and gaining momentum each step of the way.

In the Beginning

In 1994, New York–based playwright, performer, and activist Eve Ensler wrote an honest, heartbreaking, and humorous narrative based on more than two hundred interviews she conducted with a wide variety of women. The play, *The Vagina Monologues*, which was first performed in 1996 by Eve herself, received instant acclaim and many accolades (including an Obie Award), playing to sold-out houses. Eve performed the show for six months in New York, then took it on the road. After every performance, she was met by countless women who shared their own stories of surviving violence at the hands of relatives, lovers, and strangers. Overwhelmed by the number of women and girls who had experienced violence, and compelled to do something about it, she began to envision *The Vagina Monologues* as being more than a moving work of art *on* violence; it could be a mechanism for moving people to act to *end* violence.

Together with a group of New York City–based volunteers, V-Day was founded on Valentine's Day, 1998. The first V-Day was marked by a star-studded, sold-out benefit performance of *The Vagina Monologues* at the Hammerstein Ballroom in New York City. In one night $250,000 was raised and the V-Day movement was born.

V-Day began with an impressive network of well-known and talented performers who could attract broad publicity and new audiences. The word spread quickly. On February 10, 2001, a benefit performance of *The Vagina Monologues* packed the 18,000-seat Madison Square Garden, selling out and raising $1 million. The world was taking notice.

A Campus Movement

Interest was aroused on U.S. college campuses, and in 1999 V-Day launched its College Campaign. The College Campaign engaged groups of students to produce and perform benefit performances of *The Vagina Monologues,* instantly creating thousands of "accidental activists": young women and men who were thrust into the roles of gathering people to a cause, addressing groups and media about their events, and leading a team in a public-awareness and fund-raising campaign. In that first year, there were sixty-five V-Day campus productions. The campaign grew tremendously over the next five years, and in 2007 more than seven hundred colleges registered to participate.

Over the years, the College Campaign has played a significant role in building antiviolence communities on campuses by bringing together engaged, aware, and empowered women and men who are willing to stand up against violence. These activists have introduced lasting programs and activities to their campuses, such as annual weeklong festivals to celebrate violence-free zones and twenty-four-hour speak-outs to stop rape. Students at Arizona State University, for example, raised $15,000 to open Home Safe, an on-campus sexual violence prevention and education program, and SAFER (Students Active For Ending Rape) was created through V-Day activities and today is helping students to change campus policies regarding rape reporting nationwide. In many ways, the College Campaign has brought a generation of young women and men to envision a new paradigm for social action. Today it is not uncommon to see V-Day proudly listed in MySpace and Facebook profiles and on résumés of recent college grads. Being part of the V-Day movement signifies a lifelong commitment to justice for women and girls everywhere.

Going Worldwide

As the College Campaign gained momentum, word was also spreading to community activists and local theater and antiviolence groups. As a result, in 2001, the Worldwide Campaign began to take shape. Just as college students organize benefit performances of *The Vagina Monologues,* so too do communities around the world. From forty-one Worldwide Campaign events in 2001 to four hundred in 2007, the success of the campaign has been ensured by the growing list of committed and enthusiastic local groups and volunteers.

Funds raised by V-Day Worldwide Campaign organizers have saved rape crisis centers and many other organizations that work to end violence against women from closing down, or helped them to expand their services. In 2003, for example, the proceeds from a local performance of *The Vagina Monologues* in Nairobi, Kenya, helped reopen a women's shelter that had closed its doors due to lack of funding. Many V-Day activists have also helped policymakers commit to recognizing and ending violence against women and girls in their communities. Be it in rural Borneo, where rape cases are now encouraged to be heard in the civil court rather than the native court so that the rights of survivors are better represented, or in the United States, where the House of Representatives recently approved a long-awaited measure calling for an apology from Japan to the "Comfort Women,"* V-Day is

---

*The term "Comfort Women" refers to the estimated 50,000 to 200,000 girls and young women from China, Taiwan, Korea, the Philippines, Indonesia, Malaysia, the Netherlands, and East Timor who were abducted and forced into sexual slavery to service the Japanese military in "comfort stations" from 1932 to 1945.

helping to shift the culture surrounding violence against women toward accountability.

The V-Day Model Expands

As the V-Day movement grew, the elevating interest within communities hinted at the success a coordinated V-Day effort in one geographic location could yield, and several groups began to register to hold multiple V-Day events in the same cities. For an inaugural run in V-Day's hometown of New York, Eve and the V-Day team planned a two-week festival of spoken-word, performance, and community events in June 2006 called Until the Violence Stops: NYC. More than one hundred writers and fifty actors donated their talents to create four marquee celebrity events. Seventy local community events also took place, involving thousands of grassroots activists throughout the city's five boroughs. The festival brought the issue of violence against women and girls front and center across a city of eight million, inspiring V-Day to encourage its network of activists to hold festivals in other locations.

The events of the festival generated new material, resulting in *A Memory, a Monologue, a Rant, and a Prayer,* an anthology of original writings by world-renowned authors and playwrights that was released in May 2007. Another collection that came out of the New York initiative, *Any One of Us: Words from Prison,* features the writings of incarcerated women and high-lights the connection between women in prison and their own history of violence. Since the festival's debut in New York City, it has been replicated in northeast Ohio and Kentucky. The events brought V-Day's message to more than two million people in both states, raising awareness about local organizations working on the ground to end violence against women and girls. The festival will debut in Paris and Los Angeles in 2008.

Pushing the Edge

V-Day shatters taboos, lifts the veil of secrecy from the issue of violence against women, and pushes the edge. While the movement has faced resistance over the years, V-Day has always chosen to speak the truth about violence and women's sexuality rather than skirting around the issues. When Eve Ensler first performed *The Vagina Monologues,* the word "vagina" was met with controversy and discomfort. Radio stations refused to allow "vagina" to be said on the air. TV stations ran entire segments on the play without mention of the word, and newspapers hid under the safety of abbreviation. Ten years later *The Vagina Monologues* has become part of popular culture and the word "vagina" is spoken openly on TV and radio and printed freely in newspapers and magazines all over the world. With the word "vagina" being uttered and printed in mainstream media, V-Day has been a catalyst that has helped to shift culture and break through taboos so that women who have suffered invisibly in silence are forever made visible.

The resistance that V-Day has faced over the years has provided campuses and communities unique opportunities to turn negative feedback into positive dialogue among students, faculty, and community members. Resistance has also created an environment in which fixed ideas are changed, and in many cases groups end up coming together to support one another in the fight to defend *The Vagina Monologues*.

In 2005, Notre Dame University officials banned the on-campus production of *The Vagina Monologues*, sparking wide-ranging debate and resulting in a panel discussion at the university featuring members of the faculty and Eve. The following year, Notre Dame president Rev. John I. Jenkins announced that he would allow the campus production, stating, "The creative contextualization of a play like *The Vagina Monologues* can bring certain perspectives on important issues into a constructive and fruitful dialogue with the Catholic tradition. This is a good model for the future." Also in 2005, the Ugandan government shut down a production of *The Vagina Monologues* in Kampala despite the scrutiny of the international press. But activists were still able to raise $11,000 for the Lira Women's Peace Initiative and Kitgum Women's Peace Initiative, two local women's groups working to keep women safe in northern Uganda. In 2006, V-Day again found itself at the center of controversy when the president of Providence College banned the annual *Vagina Monologues* production. More than two hundred people protested and V-Day organizers from across the state of Rhode Island (as well as many of the event's beneficiaries) came to the aid of the Providence College organizers, helping to arrange an off-campus production. It continues to take place off campus.

By generating media coverage and starting a worldwide dialogue, these controversies have proven to be part of the very change V-Day seeks.

V-World

In 2001, V-Day launched a campaign called "Afghanistan Is Everywhere," through which V-Day 2002 organizers from the Worldwide and College campaigns were asked to provide information at their events in order to bring broader attention to the situation of women in Afghanistan under the Taliban. Ten percent of the proceeds from each event, totaling more than $250,000, went toward assisting the women of

Afghanistan, opening schools and orphanages and providing education and health care.

The success of that campaign evolved into what is now the annual V-Day Spotlight Campaign. Since "Afghanistan Is Everywhere," V-Day Spotlight Campaigns have included: "Native American and First Nations Women," "The Missing and Murdered Women in Juárez, Mexico," "The Women of Iraq," "Campaign for Justice to 'Comfort Women,' " "Women in Conflict Zones" (including the women of the eastern Democratic Republic of the Congo), and "The Women of New Orleans," which have raised hundreds of thousands of dollars for women in these areas and brought the issues they face into the public eye.

V-Day encourages the empowerment and leadership of local women who are negotiating change within a wide variety of local, social, political, and religious contexts. We recognize that local activists must take the lead in planning activities appropriate for the communities in which they live.

It is through the work of these local activists that V-Day comes alive in places as remote as Narok, Kenya. V-Day's work to end female genital mutilation (FGM) in the Massai community in Kenya was made possible because one Massai woman's story resonated with V-Day's philosophy. Agnes Pareyio started educating young women and girls on the dangers of FGM more than fifteen years ago. A deep friendship between Agnes and V-Day turned into a partnership that, in 2002, gave birth to the first V-Day safe house. A place where girls in Narok can go to be educated and live without fear of being cut, the V-Day Safe House for the Girls is a monumental success, inspiring women's leaders from across Africa to show interest in working with V-Day to end FGM on the continent. Today V-Day is helping Agnes build a second safe house, a place where even more girls will flourish.

In Haiti, inspired by the work of devoted and passionate women's rights activists, V-Day partnered with the Ministry for Women to build the V-Day Haiti Sorority Safe House in Port-au-Prince, the first ever long-term safe house for women in all of Haiti, which will provide shelter to women survivors from all walks of life and to their children, and will be a place of refuge where women who have been abused can be treated for trauma and also be trained for jobs. In Cap Haitien, V-Day has helped to purchase a house with a local, solely volunteer-based organization. And in Bukavu, Democratic Republic of the Congo, plans are under way to build the City of Joy, a transformative facility for 100 female survivors of sexual violence.

V-Day has seen its presence expand across the Middle East with the Karama Program, which it launched in 2005. Karama, Arabic for "dignity," supports a regional movement to end violence against women and is led by women activists from eight sectors: politics, economics, health, art/culture, education, media, law, and religion. With headquarters in Cairo and a regional office in Amman, Jordan, Karama builds networks within and across Egypt, Lebanon, Jordan, Palestine, Morocco, Algeria, Syria, Sudan, and Tunisia, providing a structure for activists in the region to come together and build the movement for women's equality and rights. In 2008 and 2009, Karama will fund the implementation of joint campaigns and self-directed action plans in each national coalition; it will also continue to support advocacy opportunities for regional delegations at UN events and in other international arenas. Because Karama has been invited into Arab women's NGOs, it is helping to build a unique coalition that will represent Middle Eastern women's voices in the pivotal decades ahead.

V10: The Next Decade

February 2008 marks the ten-year anniversary of the creation of V-Day. On the weekend of April 12, V-Day will take over New Orleans, inviting 18,000 V-Day activists to convene in the New Orleans Arena to witness and participate in V to the Tenth, a day of art, activism, and workshops to launch the next decade of our movement. Star-studded performances and a co-ordinated media effort will remind the world what V-Day has achieved since 1998 and will capitalize on the exposure to bring attention to what remains to be done. We have chosen New Orleans as the site of this significant moment in V-Day's history because the plight of the survivors of Hurricane Katrina epito-mizes what many women face around the world: high levels of violence, economic and racial injustice, and public structures that fail to protect them.

V to the Tenth will celebrate Vagina Warriors—men and women from around the world who have sur-vived and witnessed extraordinary violence, grieved it, and dedicated their lives to end violence instead of avenge it. V-Day is working collaboratively with the Katrina Warrior Network, grassroots groups in the area dedicated to helping women and girls living in and returning to New Orleans to rebuild their lives. To-gether we hope to unite, activate, involve, and trans-form the New Orleans community, forming a structure that will last through the rebuilding and beyond.

A new work created by women artists in New Or-leans and produced by V-Day and Ashé Cultural Arts Center, *Swimming Upstream,* will premiere as part of V to the Tenth, followed by a V-campaign that takes the dialogue about New Orleans broadly to thousands of colleges and communities.

V to the Tenth will also serve as a reminder and a call to action. It will prove once again that art has the power to transform thinking and inspire people to act and that lasting social and cultural change is spread by ordinary people doing extraordinary things. It will prove that local women are unstoppable, fierce leaders working to solve the problem of violence in their communities. V to the Tenth will remind the world just how far the V-Day movement has come in ten years. It will also challenge the world to take up the cause of going the distance with us, as there is still a long road ahead.

In ten years we have seen enormous transformation and very specific victories. Imagine where we will be in ten more years. With your help, we will end violence against women and girls.

We will work until the violence stops.

Please join us!

V-VOICES:

TESTIMONIALS AND THOUGHTS

FROM THE WORLDWIDE NETWORK

The Vagina Monologues *performance in Abuja and Lagos has paved the way for a movement unseen in Nigeria before now, a movement that encompasses sexual emancipation, an end to violence and a demand for equality.*
> —V-Day Worldwide organizer, Lagos, Nigeria

As one of the first to put on a V-Day in Brittany . . . I am now a member of the board of a house for battered women in my home town of Brest. . . . [I] did not know years ago [that] I would become so much involved [in] defending women's rights.
> —V-Day Worldwide organizer, Brittany, France

When I read The Vagina Monologues *in high school, I felt like I had found salvation. This was a message that every woman, man, and child needed to hear. It was truth and beauty and hope and you didn't even have to believe in God to see that. I wanted to spread it like gospel. . . . I believe that there is not a man, woman, or child who would not benefit from seeing the light of* The Vagina Monologues.

May V-Day continue until we are all converted . . . to peace.

—Tova Feldmanstern,
Why "The Vagina Monologues" Is Better Than the Bible

I am extremely angry at the Catholic organizations that malign the Monologues *and try to stop the productions on Catholic campuses. I believe the radical equality of every human being is the message that Christ came to proclaim; therefore, my appreciation of* The Vagina Monologues *in no way contradicts my Catholicism—rather, it reaffirms it. Eve has given me a new appreciation for humanity and particularly for women. . . . I'm going to do everything I can to make sure the* Monologues *are allowed on Catholic campuses [and] I'm not going to let the church forget about vaginas. I hope to be a theologian one day and I can guarantee that my theological thinking will reflect my newfound appreciation of women. I still have a lot to learn, but at least I'm on my way.*

—Joel Gray, Mississippi

She goes through it everyday
For us it's something we fear
But it's her nightmare
This pain is real
And I can't understand
What would possess a man
To cause a woman to hate herself
Make her feel like dirt
But what do you do when nothing works
No one to call
No one to tell
This is her life
Her living hell
To help this problem
We need more than the cops
So support VDAY until the violence stops

> —Emma Parker, thirteen years old

V-Day isn't a website, or a resource, or a movement. V-Day is the people who hold the goal of a world without violence deep in their hearts and their vaginas!

> —V-Day Gunnison, Colorado

Because of my work with V-Day, I was able to have a sense of strength that I'm not sure I would have had at any other time. It was hard going to the ER, and harder having a rape kit done. It was hard going to the police and naming my attacker.

I'm sure it'll be even harder in the months that follow sitting in a courtroom and reliving the experience. But V-Day and Victims Outreach gave me a sense of peace knowing that I can fight against women being treated in such a way. I don't have to be silent and I don't have to pretend that it never happened. There is a support system out there will help. So, thank you. I do feel empowered. And I hope V-Day continues to give a voice to those who have lost theirs, those who never knew they had it, and those that want to scream louder.

—V-Day organizer, University of Texas, Dallas

Thank you, you have changed another man's outlook on life, and made him more knowledgeable about how women are treated worldwide, and more committed to helping stop it.

—Michael

Every time I read a monologue, I am more proud of being a woman and knowing that I am part of a movement that has started to change the world. Thank you all for everything, for making me proud of who I am, what I am, and who I have become.

—V-Day College Campaign cast member

Standing up to the problems of rape, incest, battery, female genital mutilation, and sexual slavery is a big project socially, politically, and personally. To be a part of raising awareness, of raising money, and of raising our voices is a vital respon-

sibility of any person who calls themselves a feminist and an activist.

—Jordan, V-Day Illinois College organizer

As a lesbian, I was pleased to find that most heterosexual women had similar opinions on the vagina to me. . . . I was also glad to see lesbians recognized and defended. However, my sexuality made little difference to the way I responded to the book. I felt both individual enlightenment & a unity with women as a whole. The book made me finally realize that I am, in fact, a woman.

—Joanna

As a woman of Korean descent, I was deeply moved and grateful that The Vagina Monologues *dealt with an issue that is of great significance to the Korean people, namely, the issue of "comfort women" during WWII. . . . Also, I was inspired by how theatre has the power to educate people all around the world about issues which otherwise would not have come to our attention. Thank you, sincerely and deeply, for this once in a lifetime experience.*

—Jean

My experience in organizing the V-Day campaign in Borneo has given me so much strength, confidence, and belief in myself, and has allowed me to pursue my dream and to reach for my full potentials. I am 35 years old, a wife, and a mother to two young children. . . . I just want to say a big THANK YOU from the bottom of my heart for making a difference to my life.

—V-Day Worldwide Campaign organizer,
Kota Kinabalu, Borneo, Malaysia

If moaning on stage means that at least one other woman need not groan from hurt anymore, that one day, my sister can walk in the park without fear of being raped, that my niece can grow up in a world free from violence, then I will moan . . . and moan some more.

—Kota Kinabalu, Malaysia cast

I am involved in The Vagina Monologues *as one of many ways to repay my utang to my ancestors. The* Vagina Monologues *gathers life lessons from lolas, to nanas, to ub-bing, like stringing strands of sampaguita lei, blossom by blossom. The* Vagina Monologues *presents this lei of Pilipina voices to our present and future generations in order to honor and save lives. Be a lei maker to help the next generation and ourselves live the dreams of our sakadas.*

—V-Day participant,
Waipahu and Honolulu, Hawaii

(First-ever Hawaii intergenerational Pinay-style *Vagina Mono-logues* multilingual production in Tagalog, Ilocano, Visayan, and Pidgen English)

We did it! We received such unprecedented support from the media and the public. There was a point where anywhere you went it was The Vagina Monologues. *If you drove [down] Church Road a massive black billboard with Vagina in white sticking out meters away. If you opened the news paper it was Vagina. If you listened to the radio it was Vagina. If you switched your TV it was Vagina. . . . We sold out for both nights days before, unheard of in Zambian theatre. We had members of parliament, students . . . you name them, they were there. Even the intelligence service who were sent to check on the show forgot their duties and were enjoying themselves. We had discussions after the show, bringing out issues that have gone unspoken for generations.*

—V-Day Lusaka, Zambia

As in all the monologues, there was the initial shock of reading the word "vagina," but what was more astonishing was how exquisite the other words were. In my monologue, Eve Ensler had encapsulated not only one particular wonder of being a woman but all the emotions that it evokes. The monologue was humorous and poignant. It was raw and tender. It was beautiful. This wasn't something I had heard about The Vagina Monologues. *I knew it was supposed to be shocking, but beautiful too? . . . There were humorous monologues, empowering ones, tragic ones. Some were so familiar, I felt as though I had been their inspiration. Others dealt with concepts so foreign I was shocked I had never known about it be-*

*fore (like female genital mutilation). As a whole, the mono-
logues both educated the audience on the sorrows and dangers
facing women worldwide and reminded them of the universal
joys of womankind. Together, the monologues created a moving
portrait of what it means to be a woman.*

—Trystan, V-Day St. John's College,
Santa Fe, New Mexico

We produced The Vagina Monologues *in Spanish in this
area for the very first time! We sold out both nights and the
audience requested more presentations and a bigger venue next
year. One of our beneficiaries, Arte Sana, . . . a struggling
grass roots organization working to bring awareness in the
Latino community, really benefited from the funds in order to
pay for operation costs and thus continue to offer services.*

—V-Day Austin, Texas

*For the first time in Belgrade (and in Serbia) in one public
institution/public space [with a 600-seat capacity, which sold
out] you could hear: CUNT, VAGINA, LESBIANS, IN-
CEST, GENITAL MUTILATION, DOMESTIC VIO-
LENCE, SEXUAL VIOLENCE!!!*

*And an amazing thing happened: men were crying . . .
most of them could hardly define what happened. . . . They
understood something. There was no anger or defense."*

—V-Day Belgrade, Yugoslavia

VDAY

UNTIL THE VIOLENCE STOPS

V-Day is an organized response against violence toward women.

V-Day is a vision: We see a world where women live safely and freely.

V-Day is a demand: Rape, incest, battery, genital mutilation and sexual slavery must end now.

V-Day is a spirit: We believe women should spend their lives creating and thriving rather than surviving or recovering from terrible atrocities.

V-Day is a catalyst: By raising money and consciousness, it will unify and strengthen existing anti-violence efforts. Triggering far-reaching awareness, it will lay the groundwork for new educational, protective, and legislative endeavors throughout the world.

V-Day is a process: We will work as long as it takes. We will not stop until the violence stops.

V-Day is a day. We proclaim Valentine's Day as V-Day, to celebrate women and end the violence.

V-Day is a fierce, wild, unstoppable movement and community. Join us!

Visit our website at: www.vday.org

V - T I M E L I N E :
T E N   Y E A R S   O F   V A G I N A
V I C T O R I E S

The V-Day movement has grown rapidly in ten years. Here is a brief timeline, charting our many victories along the way.

1998

V-Day begins with a 2,500-seat, sold-out benefit performance of *The Vagina Monologues* on February 14, 1998, at New York City's Hammerstein Ballroom, raising $250,000 for local antiviolence groups. The evening features more than twenty actors, including

BETTY, Margaret Cho, Glenn Close, Eve Ensler, Giselle Fernandez, Calista Flockhart, Whoopi Goldberg, the Klezmer Women, Shirley Knight, Soraya Mire, Kathy Najimy, Rosie Perez, Hannah Ensler-Rivel, Robin Roberts, Winona Ryder, Susan Sarandon, Lois Smith, Phoebe Snow, Gloria Steinem, Marisa Tomei, Lily Tomlin, Ulali, Barbara Walters, and Chantal Westerman.

1999

V-Day holds a benefit performance in London at England's renowned Old Vic Theatre. The event raises funds for national and international NGOs that work to end violence against women. Performers included Gillian Anderson, Cate Blanchett, Sophie Dahl, Christiane Amanpour, Isabella Rosellini, Melanie Griffith, Joely Richardson, Meera Syal, and Kate Winslet. The day after the event, the actresses appear on the front pages of six London papers wearing red feather boas.

In the United States and Canada, more than sixty-six schools accept V-Day's invitation to take part in the College Campaign. According to figures reported by the participating schools, more than 20,000 people are exposed to V-Day.

2000

The College Campaign expands to 150 colleges and universities across the country and around the world (more than doubling the number of schools that participated in 1999).

2001

On February 10, V-Day sells out New York's Madison Square Garden, an 18,000-seat arena, with more than seventy actors performing. In a single evening, $1 million is raised. The audience includes finalists of V-Day's international Stop Rape Contest. The winning contestant, Karin Heisecke of Germany, proposes the "Bread Bag" Campaign, an ingenious idea to ask local bakers to wrap their bread in bags printed with statistics on violence against women and emergency contact numbers for survivors of violence.

In December, V-Day and Equality Now co-sponsor the Afghan Women's Summit for Democracy in Brussels. More than fifty Afghan women gather to define their blueprint for post-Taliban Afghanistan. Members of the group go on to collect 128,000 signatures from all 32 Afghan provinces on a petition calling for restoration of peace and disarmament. The petition is eventually delivered to UN headquarters in Afghanistan, and the UN decides to disarm 900 civilian men. V-Day commits to providing funding to the Revolutionary Association of the Women of Afghanistan (RAWA).

The College Campaign expands to 230 campuses and $620,000 is donated to local women's organizations. The Worldwide Campaign begins to take shape and V-Day events are presented in more than forty cities, raising and distributing more than $350,000 to local organizations.

2002

A V-Day celebrity fund-raiser in San Francisco raises more than $500,000 for twenty-four local antiviolence groups.

In Harlem, a star-studded cast of women of color performs *The Vagina Monologues* at the world-famous Apollo Theater. Proceeds benefit the African-American Task Force on Violence Against Women; the Dominican Women's Development Center; the Violence Intervention Program; and Sakhi for South Asian Women.

V-Day launches the Indian Country Project to raise awareness of the extraordinarily high rates of violence against Native American women. Suzanne Blue Star Boy creates twenty-five V-Day events, which take place on reservations and/or benefit Native groups in the 2003 V-Day season. V-Day funds help build a safe house on the Pine Ridge Reservation in South Dakota.

The first V-Day Safe House for the Girls, for African girls fleeing female genital mutilation, is opened in Narok, Kenya, through the work and leadership of Agnes Pareyio. It offers fifty girls a safe residential shelter and enables them to continue their schooling.

A Rome Summit in September brings together more than thirty V-Day activists from seventeen countries, including Afghanistan, Bosnia, Guatemala, Kenya, the Philippines, South Africa, and the United States, to strategize about ending violence against women and girls worldwide.

More than 514 campuses participate in the College Campaign, and the Worldwide Campaign explodes into 245 cities around the world, totaling more than 2,000 benefits in 35 countries.

2003

A V-Day public service announcement (PSA) campaign featuring star supporters and activists debuts.

Print PSAs are featured in more than thirty magazines, including *Time, Marie Claire, Spin,* and *Redbook.* The televised PSAs—produced pro bono by Lifetime Television—are broadcast more than one hundred times, reaching more than ten million viewers.

V-Day holds a summit for eighty Afghan grassroots women leaders, lawyers, activists, and teachers from thirty-five Afghan organizations in Kabul, providing them with leadership training and networking opportunities.

V-Day sponsors a conference in Sarajevo, "Crossing the Borders of Difference," bringing together women of different regional languages and loyalties into a conversation about how to find peace in a region ravaged by war and rape.

In Manila, the New Voice Company and Philippine female legislators and congressional representatives hold V-Day events for the Philippine Senate and House of Representatives to focus on domestic-violence and sex-trafficking bills. A year later, the legislation is passed.

An event in London features a cast of thirty-six disabled women, fourteen sign language interpreters, and captioners, audio describers, and access workers.

In April, grassroots activist Nighat Rizvi gathers lead-ing Pakistani actors for the first V-Day in Islamabad, Pakistan. More than two hundred people attend and the play goes on to tour Lahore and Karachi.

V-Day Lithuania is performed on the national radio station as "radio theater," a seventy-year-old tradition that many rural people rely upon for entertainment.

In December, V-Day travels to Israel and Palestine on a listening tour, meeting with women who discuss their urgent need for security, equality, justice, and peace.

More than 598 campuses participate in the College Campaign and more than 294 cities participate in the Worldwide Campaign, totaling more than 2,400 bene-fits in 38 countries.

2004

On February 14, V-Day and Amnesty International or-ganize a march of 7,500 people in Juárez, Mexico, to protest the inadequate response to the hundreds of missing and murdered women of that city. The march marks the beginning of V-Day's work to bring the world's attention to the femicide taking place in Juárez. V-Day goes on to support Casa Amiga and other local NGOs providing services and advocacy to the families of the disappeared.

A weeklong V-Day educational program organized at a high school in Amherst, Massachusetts, receives national media coverage, including *Time* magazine and the *Today* show.

Until the Violence Stops, a documentary about V-Day, premieres at the Sundance Film Festival and is broadcast on Lifetime Television in February.

Cairo audiences flock to three private sold-out performances of *The Vagina Monologues,* produced and performed by Eve, Egyptian actors, and young women from Lebanon, Qatar, and Saudi Arabia. The money raised goes to furnish a women's shelter, one of the first of its kind in the Middle East.

V-Day India celebrates the work of South Asian feminists at two sold-out gala performances of *The Vagina Monologues* featuring Indian and Pakistani actors. The performances coincide with a conference of South Asian activists from India, Pakistan, Bangladesh, Nepal, Afghanistan, and Sri Lanka. Both events are broadly covered by Indian and international news media (including *The Times of India,* the BBC, and the

Associated Press), generating massive awareness on the Indian subcontinent. V-Day helps support the opening of a sanctuary for women in Himachal Pradesh.

On March 8, *The Vagina Monologues* is performed by women MPs and ministers before a sold-out audience at the Criterion Theatre in London. More than seventy local performances are produced across the United Kingdom as well.

In April, the first transgender V-Day is staged at Los Angeles's Pacific Design Center. The women premiere a new monologue, "They Beat the Girl Out of My Boy . . . or So They Tried," based upon their stories.

With financial support from the European Commission, organizers in the United Kingdom, France, Germany, and Luxembourg establish V-Day Europe. Its goal is to support local organizers, mobilize political and public support in the EU, and develop a sustainable, expansive, multidisciplinary network in Europe devoted to ending violence against women and girls.

In June, V-Day launches a voter-registration and education campaign to get out the vote and elevate the issue of violence against women. V-Day activists in thirty-one states work to register voters to "Vote to End Violence."

More than 613 campuses participate in the College Campaign and more than 358 cities participate in the Worldwide Campaign, totaling more than 2,600 benefits in 50 countries.

2005

Ugandan authorities ban a scheduled V-Day benefit. Organizers generate national and international media coverage, raising awareness of the issue of violence against women in Africa and worldwide.

On March 8, International Women's Day, Eve and V-Day Dagur are honored at a reception at the president of Iceland's home. President Ólafur Ragnar Grímsson is given the first "Vagina Warrior President" award.

The first regional European V-Day workshops take place in April in Brussels, with fifty-five V-Day organizers representing eighteen countries. A star-studded, multicountry, multilingual production of *The Vagina Monologues* raises funding for the Rape Crisis Network Europe, Solidarité Femmes et Refuge pour Femmes Battues, and the Organization of Women's Freedom in Iraq.

On July 18, Bayat Hawa, Egypt's first safe house for women and children escaping domestic violence, opens. Created by the Association for the Development & Enhancement of Women (ADEW), the program offers comprehensive services for women and children traumatized by domestic violence, while also promoting public awareness and dialogue about violence among the media, policy makers, and community leaders.

In July, V-Day launches the Karama Program in Beirut, Lebanon, under the guidance of V-Day special representative Hibaaq Osman. Karama (Arabic for "dignity") supports a regional movement across Egypt, Lebanon, Jordan, Palestine, Morocco, Algeria, Syria, Sudan, and Tunisia to end violence against women in the Middle East. Led by women activists from politics, economics, health, art/culture, education, media, law, and religion, Karama provides a way to rebuild collaboration among Arab women's NGOs and to attract new allies.

The creator of the first V-Day Safe House for the Girls, Agnes Pareyio, is named the United Nations in Kenya Person of the Year for her fight against female genital mutilation and early childhood marriage.

On November 22, twenty-seven-year-old health and literacy worker Malalai Joya is elected to the Afghanistan parliament. Joya and V-Day join forces,

and she speaks internationally at V-Day events on be-
half of Afghan women.

More than 689 campuses participate in the College
Campaign and more than 378 cities participate in the
Worldwide Campaign, totaling more than 2,800 bene-
fits in 54 countries.

2006

V-Day joins the international call for justice and repa-
rations for "Comfort Women" (see footnote page 176).

On February 13 and 14, the V-Day Karama Program
brings thirty-five women activists from nine Arab
countries to a workshop in Amman, Jordan.

In March, Nairobi's first sexual offense bill opens for
debate in the Nairobi Parliament. The bill is drafted by
Parliament member and long time V-Day supporter
Njoki Ndungu.

In May, at the invitation of the Katrina Warriors (a network of New Orleans–based grassroots activists), more
than 1,000 people gather in McAlister Auditorium at
Tulane University in New Orleans for an evening of
storytelling and song facilitated by Eve. The evening

benefits the New Orleans Regional Alliance Against Abuse (NORAA) member organizations, igniting a community conversation about rebuilding greater New Orleans as a healthier and more secure place for women and girls.

On June 2 and 3, V-Day organizer Sampa Kangwa-Wilkie stages the first V-Day production in Lusaka, Zambia, to sold-out crowds and raises more than $4,700 for local groups. Billboards, newspapers, and radio and television stations promote the benefit widely. Members of Parliament and other notables participate in postshow discussions.

In June, V-Day launches Until the Violence Stops: NYC, a citywide two-week-long series of theater, spoken-word performance, and community events in New York City to raise awareness of violence against women and girls. The event garners strong support from the mayor's office and local businesses, the four marquee events sell out, and seventy community fundraising events are held and attended by thousands more. The city supports a public-awareness campaign on public transportation that reaches millions of city residents.

In December, Eve interviews Dr. Denis Mukwege— director and founder of the groundbreaking Panzi

General Referral Hospital in Bukavu, Democratic Republic of the Congo—to discuss sexual violence in the Congo and beyond and examine mechanisms for prevention and ways to influence policy change on the ground.

Marie Claire magazine declares V-Day the second best charity in the world, noting that 93 percent of V-Day's funding goes directly to ending violence against women and girls.

More than 693 campuses participate in the College Campaign and more than 406 cities participate in the Worldwide Campaign, totaling more than 3,000 benefits in 58 countries.

2007

In January, V-Day chooses "Reclaiming Peace" as its theme and "Women in Conflict Zones" as its spotlight campaign.

On February 21, V-Day, *Glamour* magazine and women in Hollywood gather to honor Vagina Warriors working for peace in conflict zones at a pre–Academy Awards event hosted by Cindi Leive and Paula Wagner. Rosario Dawson, Sally Field, Jane Fonda, Salma

Hayek, Marisa Tomei, and Kerry Washington co-host the event. The event honors Margaret Jayah, a survivor of sexual slavery from Sierra Leone; Myriam Merlet, the chief of staff of the Ministry for Women in Haiti; and Zoya, of the Revolutionary Association of Women of Afghanistan.

In April, Eve visits Haiti, a country beset by political violence for decades. V-Day commits to partnering with Marie-Laurence Jocelyn Lassègue, the country's minister of Women's Affairs and Rights, to open the V-Day Haiti Sorority Safe House, and supports Elvire Eugène as she purchases a safe house in Cap Haitien.

With photographer Paula Allen, Eve visits Dr. Denis Mukwege and Panzi Hospital in Bukavu, Democratic Republic of the Congo, in June. She witnesses how women and young girls who have experienced rape and traumatic fistula receive life-saving surgeries.

A Memory, a Monologue, a Rant, and a Prayer: Writings to Stop Violence Against Women and Girls is released. V-Day and the Culture Project host two readings in New York with Michael Cunningham, Kathy Engel, Carol Gilligan, Hazelle Goodman, Carole Michèle Kaplan, Michael Klein, James Lecesne, Lynn Nottage, Mark Matousek, Winter Miller, Patricia Bosworth, Elizabeth Lesser, Susan Miller, Marisa Tomei, and Olivia Wilde. Another reading by Jane Fonda, Ali MacGraw, Val Kilmer, and other renowned actors in Santa Fe benefits V-Day.

In July, the U.S. House of Representatives approves a measure calling for an apology from Japan to the surviving Comfort Women, who were bound into military sexual slavery between 1932 and 1945. The measure brings the Comfort Women a step closer toward formal recognition of their abduction and serial rape by Japanese soldiers and comes on the heels of a speaking tour of Comfort Women arranged by V-Day and the Korean Council.

The Until the Violence Stops: Northeast Ohio festival (which grew out of the Until the Violence Stops: NYC festival in June 2006) reaches more than one million people across the state, raising awareness for local efforts to end violence against women and girls.

In August, the women of the Democratic Republic of the Congo (DRC), V-Day, and UNICEF launch "Stop Raping Our Greatest Resource: Power to the Women and Girls of the Democratic Republic of Congo," a two-year campaign calling for an end to the systematic rape of women in eastern DRC and to impunity for those who commit such atrocities.

The Until the Violence Stops: Kentucky festival brings the V-Day message to venues around the state, reaching more than one million people and raising awareness about violence against women and girls.

On September 14–16, V-Day co-hosts "Women, Power, and Peace" with the Omega Institute in Rhinebeck, New York. Nobel Peace Prize laureates Shirin Ebadi, Wangari Maathai, Rigoberta Menchú Tum, Betty Williams, and Jody Williams, as well as Jane Fonda, Natalie Merchant, and many other prominent women from diverse fields gather to examine the relationship between women, power, and peace.

On September 17, Eve hosts an evening with Christine Schuler Deschryver, a tireless advocate for the women of eastern DRC at the Culture Project. Proceeds benefit V-Day and UNICEF's joint efforts to support groups working on the ground in eastern DRC.

More than 700 campuses participate in the College Campaign and more than 400 cities participate in the Worldwide Campaign, totaling more than 3,000 benefits in 58 countries.

ACKNOWLEDGMENTS

There are so many incredible people who helped give birth to this piece and then sustain it in the world. I want to thank the brave ones who brought it and me to their hometowns and colleges and theaters: Pat Cramer, Sarah Raskin, Gerald Blaise Labida, Howie Baggadonutz, Carole Isenberg, Catherine Gammon, Lynne Hardin, Suzanne Paddock, Robin Hirsh, Gali Gold.

A special thank-you to Steve Tiller and Clive Flowers for a gorgeous British premiere, and to Rada Boric for getting it done with style in Zagreb and for being my sister. Blessings on the generous, powerful women from the Center for Women War Victims in Zagreb.

I want to thank the extraordinary people at HERE Theatre in New York, who were crucial to the successful run of the play there: Randy Rollison and Barbara Busackino for their profound devotion and trust in this work; Wendy Evans Joseph for her magnificent set and great generosity; David Kelly; Heather Carson for her sexy, bold lights; Alex Avans and Kim Kefgen for their patience and perfection and for dancing the coochi snorcher dance with me night after night.

I want to thank Robert Levithan for his trust. Thanks to Michele Steckler for being there again and again; Don Summa for getting the press to say the word; and Alisa Solomon, Alexis Greene, Rebecca Mead, Chris Smith, Wendy Weiner, *Ms., The Village Voice,* and *Mirabella* for talking about the piece with such love and respect.

I want to thank Gloria Steinem for her beautiful words and for being there before me, and Betty Dodson for teaching us all about the clitoris and starting all this.

I want to thank Marc Klein for his day-to-day work and his enormous support and patience. I want to thank Carol Bodie: her belief in me has sustained me through the lean years, and her advocacy has pushed the work past other people's fears and made it happen.

I want to thank Willa Shalit for her great faith in me, for her talent and courage in bringing my work into the world, and for co-founding V-Day.

I want to thank David Phillips for being my ever-arriving angel, and Lauren Lloyd for the big gift of Bosnia. Thanks to Marianne Schnall, Sally Fisher, Feminist.com, and the V-Day Committee.

I want to thank Gary Sunshine for coming at the right time.

I want to thank my extraordinary editor, Mollie Doyle, for standing up for this book in more houses than one, and for ultimately being my great partner. I want to thank Marysue Rucci for seizing the project and helping me find its way as a book. I want to thank Villard for not being afraid.

Then there are my friends-blessings: Paula Mazur for taking the big journey; Thea Stone for staying with me; and Sapphire, for pushing my boundaries.

I want to thank great women: Michele McHugh, Debbie Schechter, Maxi Cohen, Judy Katz, Joan Stein, Kathy Najimy, Teri Schwartz, and the Betty girls for constant love and support. I want to thank my mentors—Joanne Woodward, Shirley Knight, Lynn Austin, and Tina Turner.

I want to acknowledge the brave, courageous

ACKNOWLEDGMENTS

women in the SWP program who keep facing the darkness over and over and riding through, particularly Maritza, Tarusa, Stacey, Ilysa, Belinda, Denise, Stephanie, Edwing, Joanne, Beverly, and Tawana.

I want to deeply acknowledge the hundreds of women who let me into their private places, who trusted me with their stories and secrets. May their stories lay the path for a free and safe world for Hannah, Katie, Molly, Adisa, Lulu, Allyson, Olivia, Sammy, Isabella, and others.

I want to thank Ariel Orr Jordan, who helped co-conceive this piece with me, whose kindness and tenderness were a salve, were the beginning.

Many more people have become involved in *The Vagina Monologues* since the original publication of the book.

Thank you to Joy de Menil for her insightful, passionate, and careful work on this edition, and for pushing me to write more.

Since the first publication of *The Vagina Monologues,* the play opened Off-Broadway at the Westside Arts Theatre on October 3, 1999. This production gave the play its second life.

I would like to thank David Stone, the lead producer for this production, for his extraordinary vision, tenacity, faith in *The Vagina Monologues,* and for bringing it out out out into the world. I would particularly like to thank him for jumping into the V-Day movement with both feet, and for finding a way to support the movement through ticket sales.

I would like to thank Joe Mantello for his great flair, his understated and beautiful direction, for getting me to take myself less seriously, and for convincing me to take my shoes off.

I want to thank Abby Epstein for her thoughtful, wise, and delicate ways of guiding women, and for being such a great support.

I want to thank Nina Essman for her belief in *The Vagina Monologues,* her incredible work, and for helping me find a dress.

Thank you to Eric Schnall for being such a personable, loving, smart outreach into the wider community.

I'd like to thank Bob Fennell for his grace and dignity in bringing *The Vagina Monologues* into the wider world.

I want to thank Loy Arcenas for magical vulva curtains, and for his eye for perfection and grace; Beverly Emmons for the stunning array of pinks and reds and purples, and for lighting the show in a way that made me feel both feminine and fierce.

I want to thank Barnaby Harris for dog naps, mad circles before the show, his great intensity, and his protection.

Thank you to Shael Norris for her loving hands, for labia eye shadow, for ongoing wrestling with my cowlick, and for her utter care and kindness.

I want to thank Susan Vargo for her incredible work, her lifesaving back rubs, and her great heart. Thank you to Michelle Bauer for delicious maple cookies in the middle of the winter and for making me laugh.

Many other people were responsible for the big life of *The Vagina Monologues,* both by work at the theater and outside the theater. I'd like to thank Domonic Sack, Joel Pape, Jung Griffin, Rob Conover, Arthur Lewis, Jim Semmelman, Karen Moore, Anna Hoffman, Dan Markley, Mike Skipper, The Araca Group, Amy Merlino, Patrick Carullo, Erica Daniels, Peter Askin, Terry Byrne, Eric Osburn, Russell Owen, Suzanne Abbott, Robert Fortier, Thomas M. Tyree, Jr., Marissa Yoo, Kate Sullivan, Chad Ryan Means, Charlie Chiv, Donald "Buck" Roberts, Bill Butler, David Kalodner, Tony Lipp, Josh Pollack, Gary Gersh, Larry Taube, and Sue Liebman.

I would like to thank all the actors who have generously and brilliantly performed *The Vagina Monologues.* I bless them for their great talent and their willingness and their desire to stop violence toward women.

For the Tenth Anniversary of *The Vagina Monologues*

There are so many people who are now a part of the V-Day family. I would like to thank Allison Prouty,

Tony Melchior, Joan Morgan, Amanda Martignetti and the entire staff of JFM 2, Harriet Newman-Leve, Blair Glaser, Kristen Cortiglia, Priya Parmar, Jerri Lynn Fields, Andrew Shalit, Honey Harris, Jade Guanchez, Asha Veal, Alex Petti, Cassandra Del Viscio, Wendy Shanker, Katherine Wessling, Emma Myles, Lauren Wexler-Horn, Janet Abrams, Ali Sachs, Barbara Spero, Brian McLendon, Tonda Marton, Dramatists Play Service, Sarah Vail, and Ella Golding.

To the group of women who met in my apartment in New York City in 1998 and launched the first V-Day. Who knew that it would birth this worldwide movement?

To Karen Obel for envisioning and launching the College Campaign.

To the thousands of women and men who have stood up in their colleges and communities and have shattered taboos and embraced vaginas and embodied the V-Day spirit.

To all of the donors, companies, and foundations who have grasped V-Day, not been afraid, and helped make us bigger.

To Charlotte Sheedy, George Lane and the entire CAA staff, Nancy Rose, and Frank Selvaggi for being in my corner.

To my editor Nancy Miller for her vision and faith and to Lea Beresford for her making it all happen.

To Susan Celia Swan for being in this with me

for the last ten years with all her heart, passion, and wisdom.

To Tony Montenieri for making my life possible.

I want to thank the amazing V-Day core staff—Susan Celia Swan, Tony Montenieri, Ceclie Lipworth, Shael Norris, Purva Panday, Molly Kawachi, Amy Squires, Kate Fisher, Brian Walsh, Jaune Evans, and Hibaaq Osman—for their dedication and determination to end violence against women and girls.

I want to particularly thank Hibaaq Osman for her bravery and vision of bringing V-Day to the Middle East.

Thanks also to the V-Board, who have stood with this movement and for this movement: Jane Fonda, Pat Mitchell, Mellody Hobson, Ilene Chaiken, Rosario Dawson, Cari Ross, Kerry Washington, Salma Hayek, Carole Black, Linda Pope, and Emily Scott Pottruck.

To my close friends who sustain and inspire me: Paula Allen, Kim Rosen, Judy Corcoran, Brenda Currin, Mark Matousek, James Lecesne, Clive Flowers, Diana de Vegh, Pat Mitchell, Jane Fonda, Rada Boric, Nicoletta Billi, and Marie-Cécile Renauld.

To my mother, Chris; my brother, Curtis; and my sister, Laura.

To my son, Dylan, who taught me love; my daughter-in-law, Shiva; and my beautiful granddaughters, Colette and Charlotte.

EVE ENSLER is an internationally acclaimed playwright whose works for the stage include *Floating Rhoda and the Glue Man, Lemonade, Necessary Targets,* and *The Good Body.* She is also the author of a political memoir, *Insecure at Last.* Ensler is the founder and artistic director of V-Day (www.vday.org), the global movement to end violence against women and girls that was inspired by *The Vagina Monologues.* Performances of *The Vagina Monologues,* sponsored by V-Day, have raised over $50 million to stop violence against women and girls around the world. Eve Ensler lives in New York City.